ONLY YOU ARE MINE

ONLY YOU ARE MINE

THE SACRED BOND WITH GOD

JAGADGURU SHRI KRIPALU JI MAHARAJ

TRANSLATED BY

DR SHYAMA TRIPATHI
DR KRISHNA TRIPATHI

KRIPALU BHAKTIYOGA TATTVADARSHAN

BLOOMSBURY

NEW DELHI · LONDON · OXFORD · NEW YORK · SYDNEY

BLOOMSBURY INDIA
Bloomsbury Publishing India Pvt. Ltd
Second Floor, LSC Building No. 4, DDA Complex, Pocket C – 6 & 7,
Vasant Kunj, New Delhi, 110070

BLOOMSBURY, BLOOMSBURY INDIA and the Diana logo
are trademarks of Bloomsbury Publishing Plc

First published in India 2025

ISBN: PB: 978-93-61316-13-5; eBook: 978-93-61315-95-4
2 4 6 8 10 9 7 5 3 1

Typeset in Fouriner by Manipal Technologies Limited
Printed and bound in India by Gopsons Papers Pvt. Ltd., Noida

To find out more about our authors and books visit www.bloomsbury.com
and sign up for our newsletters

Contents

Preface

THERE IS ONLY ONE spiritual principle to understand if one is to achieve the ultimate in spiritual life: You alone are mine and I am Yours. Jagadguruttam Shri Kripalu Ji Maharaj explains that the intent behind any form of devotion is simply to know and accept this. And yet, since eternity, this knowledge has eluded us, binding us to the cycle of birth and death in the form of the 8.4 million species of life. In this one-of-a-kind series that he began in 1981, Shri Maharaj Ji reveals how we can break this cycle by loving God exclusively and selflessly.

Though the subject matter is vast, Shri Maharaj Ji's summary is concise, clear and simple to understand. Topics include life after death, the relationship between food and the mind, pride, faith, grace, surrender, the nature of a genuine Saint, and more. Theories of renowned Western philosophers are discussed too, along with numerous scriptural anecdotes.

The case for change that Shri Maharaj Ji advocates is a compelling one, indoctrinating readers in the unanimous verdict of the *Vedas*, *Puranas*, other scriptures and the writings of Saints. Shri Maharaj Ji weaves a narrative that is intensely interesting, and both brilliant and logical. Though these discourses happened more than forty years ago, the content is as relevant now as it was then and will always be.

Only You Are Mine: The Sacred Bond with God is a treasure in the hands of all spiritual aspirants. By reading this book and knowing the steps to be followed for a better-balanced life, your spiritual journey will progress speedily.

Radha Govind Samiti

to be conscious. 'The mind travels faster than the wind, and yet it is made of inert *maya*?' Yes. 'That is astonishing!'

Actually, there is nothing astonishing about it at all.

Consider a towel, for example. It is inert. But when you move it by holding onto it, you will say that it is the hand that is moving it. Similarly, the mind makes the hand move, the intellect makes the mind work and the intellect receives its power from the conscious soul and performs conscious work. Thus, the presence of the soul makes the senses, the mind and the intellect work as if they are conscious. When the soul leaves the body, what you refer to as death, the body and the sense organs still exist, but they no longer function. The eyes are there, but they cannot see. The ears too are there, but they cannot hear. Thus, you have two entities, the body and the soul. Now those people who are ignorant consider the body to be *me*, whereas for the wise that *me* is the soul. The person who has not attained God, and is therefore living in a state of ignorance since time immemorial, is the person who considers the body to be the self. This is straightforward enough even for a simple-minded person to understand. But if someone still believes that he is the soul, if someone still claims this, he is absolutely wrong. If he had truly understood that he is the soul and not the body, all his worldly attachments would have ended immediately. Then how could he have feelings of attachment towards his worldly relations, towards his parents, children, and so on? How could he persist in running after the objects of the senses?

If you are a divine soul, your subject cannot be the material world of matter, because any subject must be commensurate

1

The True Relation

A KNOWER OF SPIRITUAL PRINCIPLES says, 'O God! Today I have understood that You are mine and I am Yours.' In fact, it is only this one thing that needs to be understood. There is no need to accumulate a lot of unnecessary knowledge. It has taken infinite ages to understand just this, and yet we have not truly realised that God is ours and we are His.

If one understands this truth, either now or in the future, then there will be nothing further for him to understand or attain. Does this mean that we should forcibly accept God as ours? Yes, you must.

Just consider the selfishness that exists in this world. For example, a boy comes from one place and a girl from another. They circle seven times around a sacred fire and call themselves husband and wife. Look at what deep attachment results in the world simply by the mind's acceptance. You are all familiar with the consequences that arise from this.

History bears witness to it in the love stories of Laila and Majnu, immortalised as an example of worldly love, much like Romeo and Juliet, Shirin and Farhad, and so on. All this happened through mental acceptance alone. Did Laila and Majnu's love begin at birth? No. It happened because of the mind's acceptance of the relationship.

All of you have attachments in the world. Who is less than Laila–Majnu? There are hordes of people just like you, and your love is centred somewhere or the other too — be it for your mother, son, husband or wife.

If you were not attached to anyone, then this one sentence of the Saints and scriptures that God is yours would have been enough. You would hear it, you would accept it and then love would naturally follow, and with that love, you would achieve your goal.

Yet, despite meeting countless Saints and countless descensions of God, your intellect passes the judgement 'God is not mine. My husband, wife, father, son or so-and-so insignificant worldly relations are mine.' As a result, you continue to transmigrate across the 8.4 million species of life. Until your intellect accepts God as yours above all else, nothing will be attained. All worldly relationships are just a figment of your imagination.

Your father has been your son innumerable times, your wife has been your husband innumerable times and your daughter has been your mother innumerable times. Countless times, mind you, not just ten, one hundred or one thousand times. So what is your actual relationship with them? This is just cosmic play. All these relationships are perishable and limited to a single lifetime, whereas your relationship with God is eternal and not imaginary. Yet you do not accept it. Isn't that astonishing?

Me and Mine

हरिर्देहभृतामात्मा

(Bhagavatam 4.29.50)

हरिर्हि साक्षान्द्भगवान् शरीरिणामात्मा झषाणामिव तोयमीप्सितम्॥

(Bhagavatam 5.18.13)

Our scriptures unanimously declare that the individual soul gets its consciousness from God, that is, God is the soul of every individual soul. At present, you are two — a body and a soul. The soul is that where the words 'belongs to' do not apply. For example, 'This intellect belongs to me, this body belongs to me and these senses belong to me.' Thus, you are not the senses, the mind or the intellect, because they all 'belong to me'. The statement 'My mind was confused' means that this *me* is something other than the mind. The intellect is also mine, and the mind is subordinate to it. The senses are subordinate to the mind and all of these are mine, and therefore, not *me*. Everything that constitutes *mine* serves me. This *mine* can be called the body, which consists of the material senses, the mind and the intellect. This *me* or the individual soul, on the other hand, is divine and has been declared as a part or fraction of God. This fact, that the soul is distinct from the body, is accepted even in communist countries. People say, 'Today, the prime minister, the president has left the world. Hundreds and thousands of people are going to see his body.' From this we can understand that they accept that the person who left the world was not the body. If they were truly following the tenets of Marx and Lenin, they should not have made a distinction between the body and the soul. Until the body has not been buried, they should not say that he has left the world. But they speak in exactly the same way as those who believe in the existence of the soul. The body and the possessor of the body (the soul) are therefore distinct, just as a man's wealth and the wealthy man himself are distinct. The body comprises the mind, plus the intellect and senses, which are all made of *maya*, which itself is inert, but appears

1

The True Relation

A KNOWER OF SPIRITUAL PRINCIPLES says, 'O God! Today I have understood that You are mine and I am Yours.' In fact, it is only this one thing that needs to be understood. There is no need to accumulate a lot of unnecessary knowledge. It has taken infinite ages to understand just this, and yet we have not truly realised that God is ours and we are His.

If one understands this truth, either now or in the future, then there will be nothing further for him to understand or attain. Does this mean that we should forcibly accept God as ours? Yes, you must.

Just consider the selfishness that exists in this world. For example, a boy comes from one place and a girl from another. They circle seven times around a sacred fire and call themselves husband and wife. Look at what deep attachment results in the world simply by the mind's acceptance. You are all familiar with the consequences that arise from this.

History bears witness to it in the love stories of Laila and Majnu, immortalised as an example of worldly love, much like Romeo and Juliet, Shirin and Farhad, and so on. All this happened through mental acceptance alone. Did Laila and Majnu's love begin at birth? No. It happened because of the mind's acceptance of the relationship.

1

All of you have attachments in the world. Who is less than Laila–Majnu? There are hordes of people just like you, and your love is centred somewhere or the other too – be it for your mother, son, husband or wife.

If you were not attached to anyone, then this one sentence of the Saints and scriptures that God is yours would have been enough. You would hear it, you would accept it and then love would naturally follow, and with that love, you would achieve your goal.

Yet, despite meeting countless Saints and countless descensions of God, your intellect passes the judgement 'God is not mine. My husband, wife, father, son or so-and-so insignificant worldly relations are mine.' As a result, you continue to transmigrate across the 8.4 million species of life. Until your intellect accepts God as yours above all else, nothing will be attained. All worldly relationships are just a figment of your imagination.

Your father has been your son innumerable times, your wife has been your husband innumerable times and your daughter has been your mother innumerable times. Countless times, mind you, not just ten, one hundred or one thousand times. So what is your actual relationship with them? This is just cosmic play. All these relationships are perishable and limited to a single lifetime, whereas your relationship with God is eternal and not imaginary. Yet you do not accept it. Isn't that astonishing?

Me and Mine

हरिर्देहभृतामात्मा

(Bhagavatam 4.29.50)

हरिर्हि साक्षाद्भगवान् शरीरिणामात्मा झषाणामिव तोयमीप्सितम्॥

(Bhagavatam 5.18.13)

Our scriptures unanimously declare that the individual soul gets its consciousness from God, that is, God is the soul of every individual soul. At present, you are two – a body and a soul. The soul is that where the words 'belongs to' do not apply. For example, 'This intellect belongs to me, this body belongs to me and these senses belong to me.' Thus, you are not the senses, the mind or the intellect, because they all 'belong to me'. The statement 'My mind was confused' means that this *me* is something other than the mind. The intellect is also mine, and the mind is subordinate to it. The senses are subordinate to the mind and all of these are mine, and therefore, not *me*. Everything that constitutes *mine* serves me. This *mine* can be called the body, which consists of the material senses, the mind and the intellect. This *me* or the individual soul, on the other hand, is divine and has been declared as a part or fraction of God. This fact, that the soul is distinct from the body, is accepted even in communist countries. People say, 'Today, the prime minister, the president has left the world. Hundreds and thousands of people are going to see his body.' From this we can understand that they accept that the person who left the world was not the body. If they were truly following the tenets of Marx and Lenin, they should not have made a distinction between the body and the soul. Until the body has not been buried, they should not say that he has left the world. But they speak in exactly the same way as those who believe in the existence of the soul. The body and the possessor of the body (the soul) are therefore distinct, just as a man's wealth and the wealthy man himself are distinct. The body comprises the mind, plus the intellect and senses, which are all made of *maya*, which itself is inert, but appears to be conscious. 'The mind travels faster than the wind, and yet it is made of inert *maya*?' Yes. 'That is astonishing!'

Actually, there is nothing astonishing about it at all.

Consider a towel, for example. It is inert. But when you move it by holding onto it, you will say that it is the hand that is moving it. Similarly, the mind makes the hand move, the intellect makes the mind work and the intellect receives its power from the conscious soul and performs conscious work. Thus, the presence of the soul makes the senses, the mind and the intellect work as if they are conscious. When the soul leaves the body, what you refer to as death, the body and the sense organs still exist, but they no longer function. The eyes are there, but they cannot see. The ears too are there, but they cannot hear. Thus, you have two entities, the body and the soul. Now those people who are ignorant consider the body to be *me*, whereas for the wise that *me* is the soul. The person who has not attained God, and is therefore living in a state of ignorance since time immemorial, is the person who considers the body to be the self. This is straightforward enough even for a simple-minded person to understand. But if someone still believes that he is the soul, if someone still claims this, he is absolutely wrong. If he had truly understood that he is the soul and not the body, all his worldly attachments would have ended immediately. Then how could he have feelings of attachment towards his worldly relations, towards his parents, children, and so on? How could he persist in running after the objects of the senses?

If you are a divine soul, your subject cannot be the material world of matter, because any subject must be commensurate with its enjoyer. For example, the subject of the eye is form, and the form it perceives must consist of the same materials that the eye is made of. If God were to stand in front of you, you would not see Him because He is divine, and your eyes are made of the five material elements. The eyes can only capture objects made of the same five elements. If you have truly accepted yourself to be the soul, then why would you desire to see this world, hear its sounds, and smell, taste or touch its objects? All your desires would be reduced to nothing in this regard. But this has not happened and, consequently, you are still entangled in this world of *maya*.

The Incessant Desire for Change

If I instructed the kitchen supervisor not to put any salt in the dal for three days, I would promptly start receiving complaints: 'Maharaj Ji, there has been no salt in the dal for the last three days.' I would ask, 'So what calamity has taken place?' You would say, 'I am leaving Mangarh.[1] I cannot do *sadhana* like this. I am already staying here with great difficulty because there are no chillies or spices in the food, and I am not getting the food of my choice either. And now no salt! I would rather remain at some distance from such austerity, from such a Guru and such a God.' All these attachments to the sense of taste are your own creation.

As a newborn, did you ever ask for salt? Or have you even seen or heard of a newborn asking for salt? As parents, you gradually get your child addicted to salt and tea. The child was perfectly content prior to this with the plain taste of his mother's milk. But after entering adulthood, you need all possible varieties of food. You cannot eat a meal in which only sweet dishes are served. 'Bring something salty too.' Why? Eat your fill of sweets now that they are being served. 'I get bored with one flavour.' You did not get bored even with the plain flavour of your mother's milk when you were born, but you do not remember that anymore.

The truth is that as a newborn, you could not succumb to the bad influence of your surroundings. But as you got a little older, you developed cravings for delicious dishes. We can see that all this started later; you were not born this way. As a baby, you were content and had no special demands. You drank your mother's milk and slept soundly. You would make joyful sounds and be completely devoid of all the wants and desires that you have today. Now you object to getting the same pulses or the same vegetables every day.

All of this is of your own making. From the point of view of the body, the only thing of consideration should be the usefulness of food for its maintenance. If importance is given to variety and change, then why not eat with your nose tomorrow and your ears the day after? Show your capability. Even a millionaire cannot eat with his nose or see with his ears. This incessant desire for change is a disease of your own making. You have accepted yourself to be the body and all these are ramifications of that decision.

Exclusive Attachment

In this way, even after innumerable lifetimes, we have not understood this one small thing: we are the possessor of this body – the soul – and that we eternally belong to God. The reality is that we do not want to accept that God alone is ours. A baby is told again and again that so-and-so is his mind is attached to the Supreme Power, you attain liberation and the bliss of divine love. It is that straightforward.

The condition is that our attachment should be exclusive. This exclusiveness can come about in one, two or even a thousand lifetimes, depending on your effort. You will have to practise incorporating this exclusiveness into your devotion, because you have repeatedly done nothing but tried to cheat others for your own selfish interests. Husband and wife, father and son, and master and servant spend twenty-four hours a day trying to exploit one another in order to satisfy personal self-interests. The person who is more adept at this act is more successful, but he can still never attain true peace or happiness. Even if an individual soul were to gain possession of infinite universes, this peace and happiness would still elude him.

The Restlessness

Thus, there is one knowledge that we have not acquired since beginningless time – each one of us is a soul and we have an eternal relationship with God alone. This world is meant for the maintenance of your body and not for your enjoyment. Simple food and a few clothes are all that you need. You should not desire more than this. Those who have their basic needs met are still unhappy. And those who are millionaires in this world are even more troubled!

Many people from affluent countries come running to India and roam its by-lanes looking for peace and happiness. Does it sell in the markets here? 'We have heard that these things can be attained in this country.' But you are millionaires, billionaires. 'Yes, but we cannot get a

mother. The child has no conception at this point of what a mother or father is, but these words are forced upon him twenty-four hours a day. 'This is your mother.' Finally, the poor fellow says, 'She must be my mother,' but he does not have a clue as to what it means, even at the age of five. He is told to use the word 'mother', and so he just obeys and does so. We belong to God. He is the soul of our soul. You have not been able to understand this small point since eternity, and you have always considered yourselves to be the body and not the soul. As a result, you run after the objects of the senses, because your knowledge tells you that you must satisfy their hunger. You are incapable of thinking that it is the soul's hunger that must be appeased, because you do not accept that you are the soul and, therefore, a part of God. To accept that you are a part of God, an individual soul, is to accept the straightforward fact that:

> The soul's hunger or thirst – its desire for form, sound, touch, and more – can only be fulfilled by its whole, and that whole is God.

ममैवांशो जीवलोके जीवभूत: सनातन:। (*Gita* 15.7)

The individual soul is an eternal part of God. This is not an imagined truth, something that is only applicable for a few days or in a single lifetime. This is an eternal truth. Ever since God has existed, so has this relationship. We just have to accept this one fact that He alone is ours. But you should not think, 'God alone is mine.' Instead, you should think, 'God is also mine.' When you go to a temple, you utter the verse, त्वमेव माता च पिता त्वमेव। What is the meaning of this verse? 'You alone are my father. You alone are my mother.'

The word 'alone', *eva*, is used. When you say alone, you cannot then accept anyone else as your mother. There is this condition of exclusiveness. However, because you love both God and this world, your relationship with Him has *also* mixed up in it. You say to Him, 'You are also mine, and the world is also mine.'

The condition specified by God in this regard is: 'I will assume your full responsibility when you accept only Me as yours.'

मामेकं शरणं व्रज। (*Gita* 18.66)
योगक्षेमं वहाम्यहम्॥ (*Gita* 9.22)
तेषामहं समुद्धर्ता। (*Gita* 12.7)
अहं त्वां सर्वपापेभ्यो मोक्षयिष्यामि। (*Gita* 18.66)

All these responsibilities that He assumes, such as preserving what you have, providing you with what you lack and protecting you from the results of sin, and so on, apply only to those who consider Him alone as theirs. This rule is not for those who have applied 'also' in their devotion.

Suppose a married woman in this world accepts another man as her husband and tells her actual husband, 'You are also my husband.' Her husband would say, 'What do you mean "also"?' She would answer, 'Yes, I have another husband,' to which he would reply, 'Then get out of my house!'

You do not have the courage to use 'also' even in worldly relationships, and this is a major illusory relationship between a man and a woman, simply strengthened by going seven times around a fire! But even here, you do not use 'also'. And with God you say, 'You are *also* mine,' because to say 'alone' implies ending attachments in the world, and you do not want

to do that. Some people ask if they can keep their worldly attachments intact and attain God at the same time. This is impossible and can never happen because we attain what we have surrendered to. If you are attached mentally to the world, then you will attain the world. If your mind is attached to the Supreme Power, God, then you will attain Him.

यान्ति देवव्रता देवान्पितॄन्यान्ति पितृव्रताः।
भूतानि यान्ति भूतेज्या यान्ति मद्याजिनोऽपि माम्॥ (*Gita* 9.25)

This is clearly stated in the *Gita*: 'Whomsoever you love and are attached to in this life, after death you will attain their personality.'

Three sisters were married to three brothers who were all college graduates. The first brother was selected for the administrative services and went on to become a collector. The second brother could only become a clerk, and the third, falling into the company of drunkards and gamblers, could not get a job and became a beggar. Now how will the three sisters be addressed? The wife of the collector will be addressed as madam. The wife of the second brother will be called the clerk's wife, and the third brother's wife will be addressed as a female beggar. Although the three sisters have the same background, the same mother, they all are now in different situations.

Similarly, our mind is just like these girls. If the mind gets attached to somebody or something *tamasic*, you attain hell. If it finds some form of attachment with a *rajasic* person or thing, then you achieve the earthly region. If it is attached to a *sattvic* personality or thing, you attain celestial abodes, which are also temporary, like this material world. If the same

good night's sleep.' They need sleeping pills to sleep. This is the condition of those with excess money, and yet you covet this state? 'No, that will not happen to me. If I earn a million dollars, I will sleep peacefully.' This is an illusion.

The more you get of this world, the more your desires increase and the more dissatisfaction you feel. I have associated a lot with the wealthy and powerful, including the officer class and wealthy industrialists. If you could enter their hearts and minds and see their pitiable condition, you would never desire their position and instead be perfectly satisfied with where you are.

You all can freely roam around any time of the day or night, but what about this billionaire? Unless he has his two or three armed bodyguards to escort him, he cannot go out for fear of his life. And this is just one of his problems! Such a person has so much fear. The level of fear that exists in affluent countries is higher. You keep hearing and reading about the creation of the neutron bomb today and some other bomb the next. These weapons are all created out of fear, not with the intention of ever using them. They are created to instil fear into the minds of the opposing party. The primary reason for creating these is that people are fearful themselves and want protection.

Superficial Acceptance

In this way, you must understand one hundred per cent and with full realisation that the only relation of the individual soul is God. Let me explain to you the means to realise it. When a man who has not eaten for four days is about to eat, and someone tells him that there is poison mixed in the food, that starving man will immediately believe it and refrain from eating. Has he seen anyone putting poison in the food? No. 'Then how do you accept it?' He would say, 'That person said so.' You immediately put so much faith in some third person. But the eternal message of the scriptures, that God alone is yours, falls on deaf ears. You will not accept the truth, but you are ready to immediately accept any bogus news you hear.

A man goes running through a neighbourhood shouting that multiple stabbings have taken place, when in fact nothing of the sort has happened. The people who hear it start running. One says, 'Twenty-five people were killed!' Now the collector is worried, and the police force becomes tense running back and forth. But upon further inquiry they discover that it was just a hoax.

One man's story causes this entire disturbance, and everyone accepts it. But to accept divine truth is very difficult. If you were to accept what is one hundred per cent true, even for once, your ultimate goal would be achieved. But here you harbour doubt. 'I am highly educated, holding an advanced academic degree. How can I blindly accept something like that?'

In matters relating to God, we use all kinds of arguments, logic, reasoning and verbal sophistry, but in matters relating to this world, we have blind faith.

You experience this every day. For example, if the media announces the death of a minister or president, you automatically accept it. If they retract their statement a little later and announce that the person is alive – well, you accept it again!

In fact, you can accept anything in the world, but you have great trouble accepting the verdict of scriptures and instead have all kinds of doubts about something that is an absolute fact. You have only to accept one thing, which is that God alone is yours, because you are the soul and not the body.

The body is *mine*. We can see during the time of someone's death that this *me* leaves and the *mine*, that is, the dead body, stays behind. When thousands attend the funeral of some renowned person, they say they are going for his final *darshana*. But he is dead. 'Yes, yes. We are going to see the body,' they say. In other words, the individual soul has gone. 'So the soul and the body are different?' Yes, and you are the soul, not the body.

Dissatisfaction and Unfulfillment

The soul is divine and therefore it cannot be perceived even by great scientists adopting the most sophisticated techniques. Scientists have enclosed a dying man in a sealed glass box hoping to see the soul as it leaves the body and attempted various other things too, but all to no avail. No one has been able to perceive the soul through any material means.

The soul is extremely subtle and, being a part of God, it is divine. It is only upon attaining God that we will attain the peace and happiness for which the soul is eternally hankering, and the soul will then experience true satisfaction. If you do not attain it, then even infinite material pleasures experienced daily through worldly relations, social status, wealth, fine foods, or anything else will still not satiate you. In this way, everyone will remain dissatisfied.

An MLA wants to be a minister, a minister wants to be a chief minister and a chief minister wants to be the prime minister. Everyone remains troubled because desires never come to an end. A sub-inspector in the police force feels there can be nothing lacking in the post of a deputy inspector general, but the deputy inspector general himself is coveting the post of an inspector general! Where will it end? Indra, the king of the celestial abodes, desires Brahma's position! Even he is dissatisfied, unfulfilled and feels incomplete. This is not the cure for this disease. If you pour clarified butter onto a fire, the flames will just double in intensity instead of extinguishing.

The Triad

Thus, we have now understood that God alone is mine and I am His and *maya* is a separate entity. The world is created by *maya* and so is our body.

The world is for the body and God is for the soul. There are separate relationships; the world is for its use and we are God's and He is ours. The moment this knowledge becomes firmly established in our mind, we will start loving Him without exerting any effort.

Knowing leads to acceptance and acceptance leads to love. Suppose there is an officer's servant who has been approached by a beggar asking for alms. He pleads, 'Give me some food and I will give you this *parasa*, touchstone, in return.' The servant has never seen a *parasa* before, nor does he know what it can do, but he has heard that it is very valuable. He thinks to himself, 'I will feed this beggar food in exchange for the touchstone which I will present to my master. He will be happy to receive it, and my job will be more secure.' With this in mind, he gives the beggar some food and accepts the touchstone in exchange.

When his master returns home, the servant tells him the story and gives it to him to make him happy. The master chastises him: 'You fool! If it really is a touchstone, why would he be begging for food from you? You do not have even this common sense?' Saying so, he throws the stone out of the window. The stone touches an iron bolt and the bolt instantly turns into gold. The master stares at the gold bolt. He then touches the *parasa* to some other iron objects and they all turn into gold. He becomes overwhelmed with joy. 'I no longer need a job as I can have as much gold as I want.'

Now observe. When the officer did not know the stone was a touchstone, he did not accept it, that is, he had no love for it. However, when he knew and accepted it to be a touchstone, he became attached to it and kept it safely under lock and key. In this way, he fell in love with it immediately. Knowing, accepting and loving all happened simultaneously. In the same manner, you have similar experiences in the world.

A girl is walking down the street and a boy is passing her by on his bicycle, staring at her. The girl looks at him angrily, ready to hit him. The boy goes on by. Her close friend then says, 'What are you doing? This boy has been chosen by your parents to marry you.' The girl says, 'Really?' Now she looks at him stealthily.

What happened here? She was ready to hit him at first and now she is so joyful just from stealing a glance at him. Now there is a feeling of affinity.

Wherever there is self-interest, there is attachment. This is a straightforward fact.

जा ते कछु निज स्वारथ होई। ता पर ममता करै सब कोई॥ (*Ramayana*)

This is a natural law. All attachment is based on self-interest. When you realise that your true self-interest lies in God, you will not need to practise loving Him. There will be instantaneous love. But because you have accepted the world as yours for a long, long time, you will have to practise erasing this, which is what is taking time. One moment you accept God as yours, and then the mind takes you back into the world because of its prolonged practice of thinking in this way.

There are some people who are so addicted to cigarettes that they feel troubled even during my one-hour lecture. 'Oh, when will it be over so that I can go out and have a smoke?' A little while ago, I had caught a fellow with a huge moustache sitting and smoking. Such a person cannot immediately renounce a habit like smoking just by coming to the *satsanga*. Just think, a mere inert material object like a cigarette can enslave you in this way. If you loved God, you would receive the bliss of divine love, which is infinitely greater than the smoke of any cigarette. How could you then think of the world?

The True Relationship

You need to practise detaching yourself from the things you have had past practice in thinking about. The scriptures have been made for this reason — to give us the method and means to divert the mind to God. All the scriptures, the various paths and the various Saints stress on one thing: accept Him alone as yours, because He alone is in fact yours.

This is not something imaginary that you should just believe in, like some worldly relationship. This is an actual fact which should never be doubted. It is the world and worldly relationships that should be doubted, but this is where you have faith, and you doubt God. How topsy-turvy your knowledge is! We must accept that God alone is ours and we belong to Him. This relationship is indisputable; we have forgotten it, but He has not.

साक्षी चेता केवलो निर्गुणश्च ॥ (*Shvetashvatara Upanishad* 6.11)

The *Vedas* state, 'He resides within our heart noting each and every idea of each and every moment.' As a father, He performs His duty without expecting any salary in return, and without any verbal or written request made by you to Him to manage your account. And it is not that He only keeps the accounts for His devotees and not fallen souls. God says, 'It does not matter how fallen you are, after all, you are My child. I will keep track of all your activities and give you the fruits [of your actions] without you needing to ask and without any salary.' In the world, if you employ even an ordinary accountant you will have to pay him a fixed amount as salary. And God is keeping your account and notes each idea of every moment and does not renounce you for a second.

He is always standing right behind you and remains expectant that you will turn towards Him one day, either by a right about-turn or a left about-turn, or in any other way, and that you will *surrender* to Him so that He can assume full responsibility of you and free you (from the bondage of *maya*) forever. He wants to bestow upon you the wealth of His divine love, His infinite bliss. But you will have to love Him alone to receive it.

But how should you love Him? What is the method of becoming exclusive in your love for God?

2

The Mind and the Intellect

THE *VEDAS* STATE THAT the soul is a part of God, it is His servant and is eternal.

चिन्मात्रं श्री हरेरंशं सूक्ष्ममक्षरमव्ययम्।
कृष्णाधीनमिति प्राहुर्जीवं ज्ञानगुणाश्रयम्॥ (*Vedas*)

The individual soul is said to be made of pure consciousness,
a subtle, imperishable and eternal fragment of the Lord.

We have heard this infinite times since time immemorial but have never accepted it as a fact. We have heard it a lot, read it a lot, agreed to it and even claimed to understand it, but we have not accepted. The reason for this is that in the course of our past innumerable lifetimes, we have accepted this world to be ours, and as a result, we are unable to break this habit. This is the problem.

It is not that we are stubbornly insistent on accepting *mayic* personalities as ours and denying our true relationship with God, but the bad practice from the past prevents us from accepting it now, even though we know everything. This is our great misfortune. Having encountered innumerable Saints and descensions of God, having studied the scriptures innumerable times, having been given commentaries on the *Vedas* countless times, having held posts like that of Indra, the king of the celestial abodes, millions of times and having received every type of knowledge, we still have not accepted God as ours. This is essentially due to incessantly thinking over infinite lifetimes that this world is ours. This ingrained past thinking continues to act as a stumbling block.

There is a story of a Hindu who converted to Islam. The maulvi told him to take the name of Allah and Khuda and forbade him from saying Rama and Shyam. He agreed, but when he would wake up in the morning and stretch, he would say Rama because he would forget that he was now a Muslim. On being chastised by the maulvi, he said, 'Lord Rama has been in my heart for forty-two years and Khuda only entered yesterday. How can I get rid of Him so soon?'

Things will take time and you will have to practise for a good length of time. When Rama, who has been in the heart for forty-two years, does not change into Khuda overnight, this world that has been in your heart since eternity will not be eliminated simply by the sayings of one, two or even ten Kripalus! You will have to exert concerted effort and do your *sadhana*.

Having understood that God is mine, the question now arises, 'What must be done in order to accept Him as such and to reject this world?' The fact that the world is not mine is visible even to the greatest fool. You may go around a fire seven times and become husband and wife, and after that, if either the husband or wife dies, what will happen to the vow 'till death do us part'? 'Oh, that was my death, not yours, because yours is not in my control and when my time comes, I will have to leave.' Now in your next life, there will be another wife or husband, another father and mother, and so on, and a new chapter will begin. This drama has been enacted countless times. Now we must reflect on the solution.

The Inner Machinery

Who must consider God alone as his? You must remember that I have said that there are two interpretations of the word 'me'. The first 'me' is the individual soul, and the other 'me' is this body, including the senses, mind and intellect. Now who is the doer of all activities? If it is the soul, then why have such bad days befallen us?

The soul is a non-doer, yet it must suffer the consequences of actions.

Samkhya philosophy states that the soul is a non-doer, but that is not actually so.[1] If it were, then it would have stated, 'The soul is a non-doer and nature is the doer.' The philosophy of Nyaya says that the mind and the intellect are associated with the soul, but Samkhya says that the soul is detached. If the soul was detached and a non-doer, how could it be revolving and suffering in the form of the 8.4 million species of life? This means that the soul is a doer and does experience happiness and distress. Though it is eternal, all these adjuncts accompany it.

Not even a single thought or action of ours is separate from the soul. This remains the case until God-realisation is attained. Once we attain God-realisation, the mere vision of Him will put an end to all these afflictions. This is also stated in the *Mundaka Upanishad* (2.2.8).

Thus, the inner machinery, *antahkarana*, consisting of the mind, the intellect and *samskaras*, the tendencies of the mind caused by one's actions in their past lives, will accompany the individual soul even after death.

The doer of all activities is this *antahkarana*, the mind and the intellect, but it is linked to the soul. The *antahkarana* on its own is *mayic*, inert and works only upon receiving power from the individual soul. Without this power, the mind is as inert as this dust, that is, it is completely lifeless. Let us understand this *antahkarana* in more detail.

Antahkarana means the internal machine. The word *antah* means 'internal' and *karana* refers to 'the machine with which things are done'. This *antahkarana* is a single word denoting a single thing which manifests in two ways — *mana* (mind) and *buddhi* (intellect). However, the followers of Samkhya consider three aspects — *mana, buddhi* and *ahankara* (ego). On the other hand, the Advaita Vedantists consider four aspects — *mana, buddhi, chitta* (the reasoning faculty) and *ahankara*. In short, it can be said to be two — *mana* and *buddhi* — and this is how the *Gita* describes it.

मय्येव मन आधत्स्व मयि बुद्धिं निवेशय। (*Gita* 12.8)

Fix your mind exclusively on Me, and let your intellect also
be absorbed in Me.

मय्यर्पितमनोबुद्धिः। (*Gita* 12.14)

One whose mind and intellect are offered to Me (God).

This *antahkarana* is therefore a combination of the mind and intellect. Now what does the mind do? The mind first grasps the objects of the senses — sights, smells, sounds, tastes and tactile sensations – with the help of those senses. The senses cannot work if the mind is involved elsewhere. For example, suppose some of you are sleeping during the lecture or *kirtan*, and your mind is dreaming. In this state, your ears will not hear. The mind's work is the main thing, but it takes the support of the senses to perceive worldly objects. Having done that, there is an analysis of the available options based on past recollections.

For example: Is this person I am seeing a man or a woman? Should there be attraction, neutrality or aversion towards this person? Are they favourable or unfavourable? Would my self-interest be helped or harmed by this interaction?

Now the mind stops its work and sends the relevant information to the intellect, the central government, for a final judgement, and it says, 'This person is no one known to you, move on.'

When you walk around in the market, you see thousands of people, places and shops, and when you see a friend, you feel happy and say, 'Hello, when did you arrive?' This happens because the intellect had instructed the mind, 'This person is your friend.' The mind then tells the senses, 'Speak to him properly. He is someone dear to you.' The intellect had not given this sort of instruction previously when you were seeing all those thousands of other people, because you had nothing to do with any of them.

From this, we can conclude that the mind does two things. First, it analyses the situation and sends information to the intellect for a final decision, based on the information at hand. It then issues the order to the senses about how to speak, see, walk or act, which you then perform accordingly, be it towards your enemy or friend.

The mind grasps the objects via the senses. Then it sends this information to the intellect. The intellect now sends its decision to the mind, then the mind gives the order to the senses and the senses interact with that object. This is the sequence of events that takes place in your inner machinery, the *antahkarana*, which occurs at every moment, which you are unable to properly comprehend, and which goes on regardless. This sequence is the same for an illiterate man and for gigantic intellects like those of Brihaspati and Sarasvati.

The Decision

Someone who knows philosophy also uses this same sequence. His mind will look at the world and send information to the intellect, but because his intellect is guided by his Guru's teachings, it will give the correct decision: 'this is not yours, so do not take your mind and senses there.' His senses, too, will not object. They are inert servants of the mind, just as a horse's main concern is not where he is going, as he goes according to the whim of the rider. Similarly, a car goes wherever the driver takes it.

The mind offers no resistance; it simply follows the intellect. That is why the power of discrimination (*viveka*) is essential — right understanding must be cultivated. From countless lifetimes, your deeply rooted inner conviction has been: 'this world is mine.' People keep chasing worldly attachments, if not their own spouse or children, then someone else's — adopting, attaching, clinging in new ways. Even after retirement, this pursuit doesn't stop. Because a deluded intellect urges them to remain entangled in the *mayic* world and never break free.

I explain to people, 'Now that your son has grown up and is earning a living for himself, you should let him take responsibility for himself and make yourself free.' 'But he is still only a child,' they say. 'What do you expect, that he grows up and becomes your father? He will always be a child in your eyes. If not now, when will you start working for your own spiritual welfare?' This decision is made by the intellect, which itself is *mayic* and has eternally engaged in the erroneous practice of siding with *maya*. Such a person can never move towards God. This is only possible for someone who has surrendered his intellect to his Guru. That is why Shri Krishna proclaims in the *Gita* that two things must be surrendered.

मय्येव मन आधत्स्व मयि बुद्धिं निवेशय। (*Gita* 12.8)

In the *Gita*, Shri Krishna says, 'Arjuna, give Me your mind.' Arjuna thinks, 'Never mind. The main power, my intellect, is still in my hands. I will hand over my mind.' Shri Krishna immediately understands this and says, 'Give Me your intellect too.'

To do this is to *surrender* everything. You have neither this world nor the next; everything comes to an end because you commit to act according to the person to whom you hand your intellect. If it is someone from another world, he will take you there. If it is someone from this world, he will bring you here, and if he is a drunkard, a gambler or a meat-eater, then he will take you to the lower, hellish regions. Wherever you *surrender* your intellect, you will get the consequence accordingly. Everything depends on the intellect, so you must be extremely cautious until your intellect is *vyavasayatmika* or decisive. This intellect becomes decisive only on the direct perception and experience of God and not before. Until you have attained the bliss of divine love, you are in danger of a downfall. Do not consider yourself so advanced that you can ignore this danger.

The Line of Safety

Let us say that it is possible for you to safely cross 190 metres of a 200-metre-wide stream in a boat, but due to carelessness, you decide to try and jump the last ten feet. You have to reach the bank, and you might drown before you do.

You must have played or watched the game of kabaddi. There is a line drawn between two opposing teams. One player goes to the opponent's side and must touch one of their players and then touch the intermediate line, all within a single breath. If an opponent touches him before he touches that line, that person is considered the loser. He therefore remains in danger until he touches the line.

In the same way, until we touch God, until we realise God, we are in danger.

भावोऽप्यभावमायाति कृष्णप्रेष्ठापराधतः ॥

(*Bhakti Rasamrita Sindhu* 1.3.54)

Even those at an advanced stage of *bhakti*[2] can lose everything if they are not extremely vigilant. So ordinary spiritual aspirants should not develop the pride that they understand everything, and nothing can disturb them. It's like dealing with snakes. We are not expert snake charmers who can meddle with snakes and remain unaffected by their venom. A snake charmer uses various concoctions through which he can neutralise the effect of the snake's venom. If you were to attempt such an act now, you would be finished in the first attempt itself!

The Stumbling Blocks

Thus, it is this intellect which is the main concern, and it has deprived you of your ultimate goal for endless lifetimes. This intellect is of many kinds, but essentially, it can be categorised in two ways. We can call it the correct and incorrect intellect. Samkhya philosophy terms it as the *sattvic* and *tamasa* intellect. The *sattvic* intellect has four qualities – *dharma, jnana, vairagya* and *aishvarya*. The *tamasa* intellect has the four opposite qualities – *adharma, ajnana, avairagya* and *anaishvarya*. The *Yoga Darshana* describes these four negative qualities as *panchaklesha* or the five afflictions – *avidya, asmita, raga, dvesha* and *abhinivesha*. These five miseries have afflicted us since eternity.

The qualities of a *tamasa* (or incorrect) intellect are:

Adharma or Abhinivesha

What is called *adharma* in Samkhya philosophy is called *abhinivesha* in the *Yoga Darshana*. This *abhinivesha* is the desire to not die. This fear of death troubles you. When you see a revolver or a snake, you say, 'Oh, I will die!' But you are the soul and cannot die. It is the body that must die, because it is perishable.

You have seen throughout history that even the greatest yogis, sages and ascetics have all perished. Such people could ascend to the celestial abodes or descend to hellish regions at will. What is so special about your body that makes you think that you will not die? 'No, the body will have to perish.' Then why are you afraid? 'I know all this, but I am fearful nevertheless.' This is called *abhinivesha* in the *Yoga Darshana* and *adharma* in Samkhya philosophy.

Adharma means to forcibly accept something which is not true or worthy of acceptance and obtain grief over it. We want to hold onto the body, even though we see death snatching away the people around us daily. I have often told you about the 60 questions that the *yaksha* put to Yudhisthira. The most important one was: 'What is the most astonishing thing in this world?' Yudhisthira replied, 'Humans as well as other living beings are dying daily. Some die at birth, some in their youth and some in old age. But those who are left behind consider themselves to be here permanently and try to avoid death.'

अहन्यहनि भूतानि गच्छन्तीह यमालयम्।
शेषा: स्थिरत्वमिच्छन्ति किमाश्चर्यमत: परम्॥ (Mahabharata)

Everyone is fearful of death. Everyone knows they must die, but no one wants to. Do you feel you have the power to start planning how to circumvent God's law? 'No, no, we do not desire to do any planning, nor are we capable of doing it.'

When great sages, ascetics, yogis and even celestial gods, who consume *amrita* to remain immortal, cannot break God's laws, where do we stand? In the celestial abodes, they have *amrita* — Kamadhenu and Kalpavriksha. Why can't the celestial gods wish to never die? Their lives are limited, too. The king of the celestial abodes, Indra, has a lifespan of a hundred celestial years, after which he too is forced to vacate his seat and descend into some lower species. Even Brahma has a limited lifespan! There is a saying in English, 'dead sure', which means something is as certain as death. When it is certain, why worry about it?

Night follows day without fail, and we're not troubled – it's expected. Death, too, is natural, so why do you fear and resist death? It is not just youthful people; even elderly or disease-ridden people – whom no one cares for anymore, who are unable to get up from bed – are fearful of death. Although death could bring them some relief from their present suffering, they still object. 'I have to see my grandchild marry.' But hasn't he already witnessed enough – his own wedding and his son's? What more will he gain by witnessing another marriage? Just another moment added to endless worldly attachments.

This is *abhinivesha*, and this misery afflicts everyone who considers themselves to be the body. If you consider yourself the immortal soul, then this will come to an end. When the body is perishable, why fear death? When the time of death is also fixed, why be troubled over it? But you see fear everywhere.

I was once flying from Delhi to Nagpur when the plane's engine failed, and we had to turn back. At that time, the passengers' expressions were worth seeing. 'Oh! Now we are finished!' What will happen with death? Will you become any less? You are leaving the body, which is nothing new for you. You get this body in your mother's womb, and you will get another one. If you say that so-and-so lost a human body and that he will not get one so easily again, then you should have thought of that earlier and done things to guarantee a human birth.

Ajnana or Avidya

You all know *ajnana* or lack of understanding. This is termed *avidya* in *Yoga Darshana*.

Avairagya or Raga-Dvesha

What Samkhya refers to as *avairagya* is referred to in *Yoga Darshana* as *raga-dvesha*. *Vairagya* means 'without attachment'. In *Yoga Darshana*, they mention two things – love and hatred. To be without both of these is *vairagya*, so both are correct. What happens in love, *raga*?

Attachment of the mind. There is favourable attachment, like that towards your mother, father, son, and so on, and unfavourable attachment, like you have towards an enemy. Your enemy also dwells in your mind twenty-four hours a day. There is no difference in the result of these two emotions.

When you think of a loved one, such as your son, you think of his eyes, nose, mouth, his manner of walking, etc. You think of your enemy in the same way – that rascal, with that type of moustache. Thus, there is mental attachment in animosity too. And, of course, there is attachment when the thinking is favourable too. My point is that the reaction to both is the same – the personality of the person you love or hate permeates your heart. This is the result.

When we are attached to someone, his loving memories, even in separation, cause the heart to melt.

When we remember a Saint or God, our heart melts; they permeate the heart and purify it too. When the heart melts for a *sattvic*, *rajasic* or *tamasic* personality, be it your husband, wife, father or son, those qualities also permeate your heart. In other words, we acquire the quality of the person our heart melts for – the person we are attached to. Everyone in this world is impure because of being under *maya*. Therefore, whoever we love, be it our father, wife or son, it does not matter. We will receive the qualities of that person in our mind, just as wax that is mixed with colour becomes pervaded by that colour and both become inseparable. In the same way, the mind that is moved by the emotion of love or animosity towards anyone attains the form of that person. Detachment, therefore, means to be free from both attachment and aversion.

Anaishvarya or Asmita

The next quality referred to in Samkhya philosophy is *anaishvarya*, which is called *asmita* in *Yoga Darshana*. This refers to the ego. Everyone is bothered by their ego. 'I am someone. The person next to me is a fool. He does not know how to sit properly. He does not know how to speak.' What is this problem that you all have? You cannot sit properly in a train or bus without putting on a show, without any reason for doing so. The poor fellow sitting next to you is not saying or doing anything, but you act reserved and your manner of sitting, looking and speaking is very artificial. Why does this happen? There is this demon within you called the ego which makes you do all this. Are you comfortable doing this? 'No, but what can I do? I get these orders from within. I am most comfortable when I am all alone at home, behind closed doors with absolutely no one. Then I do not care how my clothes look or where my hands and legs are; I am in my own natural state. But the moment someone comes in, I have to behave. I am mindful of my attire and sit properly, lest someone says something.' Thus, there is nothing natural in this state. This is the ego.

The Driver

I am trying to make a single point: it is due to the order given by the intellect that we perform all our work. Then what are we to do? We have to consider God as ours and not the world. What causes the problem with this is, therefore, the intellect and not the mind. The poor mind is unnecessarily being chastised. For example, when a car accident takes place, it is the driver who is taken to task and not the car, because the driver has made the mistake. Likewise, the senses and the mind are merely instruments in the hands of the intellect and whatever they do is the intellect's fault. Someone may say that he has less intelligence, but why? Because that person has not met anyone with proper intelligence, and even if he has, he still considers himself more intelligent and therefore he doesn't change. In other words, whenever we meet a Saint, due to our faulty intellect, we cannot receive any benefit. Our intellect tells us that we are perfectly all right where we are. In trying to understand a Saint, our intellect says that it is not ready to accept anyone as being greater, nor is it ready to *surrender* or implicitly follow the teachings of the Saint. The mind functions in combination with the intellect, and we refer to this pairing of the mind and the intellect as the mind. This is what the *Gita* states.

Here, the mind refers to the mind and the intellect. As I mentioned earlier, the inner machinery, or the *antahkarana*, is one, but according to its state of work, it is referred to as the mind and the intellect. Just as our present actions become our destiny, so too can these two things of ours be referred to as two states, which are called by different names.

The mind and the intellect are two specific states of one inner machine, the *antahkarana*. For this reason, various Saints are only seen chastising the mind. In such instances, they are referring to the mind and the intellect. It is this machine in its entirety that must be connected to God, and the prerequisite for this is that one needs to understand that this world, which it is currently attached to, is not ours. And that is something you have not yet understood.

Speeding Away

At present, we are moving with full intensity towards the material world, becoming increasingly entangled in *maya*. If only we had paused for a moment, and someone had guided us to turn left, right or completely around, we would have done so without resistance. But the problem is that we never stop.

न हि कश्चित्क्षणमपि जातु तिष्ठत्यकर्मकृत्। (Gita 3.5)

We are constantly moving and moving at such a fast pace that it is not possible for us to be inactive even for a moment, and we are therefore constantly moving in the wrong direction and towards the world. The decision of the intellect is constantly taking us in this direction. The first thing to do, then, is to stop.

If someone asks you, 'Hey, listen, where are you going?' You will say, 'To my home.' They will reply, 'But your home is not here!' You will say, 'I don't have time for all this useless talk. I am going full speed in the direction everyone else is going.' They will say, 'But your destination is not in that direction.'

'Everyone is going the opposite way to you (towards the world); are they all fools?'

It is just a handful of people, Saints like Tulsidasa, Surdasa, Mira and Kabira, who say that our actual home is in the other direction. Everyone else says it is right here in this world. They say that if you become a millionaire, you will attain bliss. Thus, everyone is going forward with such speed that no one has time to stop and listen.

'I have come to explain the goal of life to you.'

'That's all right, sir, but I just do not have the time.'

You have all the time in the world to run, but no time to hear or understand in which direction you have to run! There is a firm decision that has been made to listen to everybody but to do what the mind says.

People will listen to a Saint and even nod their heads to make him happy, but when it comes to their inner thoughts, they think, 'Do not fall into all this foolishness. You have to become a millionaire if you want real peace. Only then will you be able to sleep in peace.' You must first free your mind of all attachment and aversion to this world. In other words, you have to reduce the speed at which you are running towards the world. When you drive a car, the greater the curve, the more you reduce your speed. Similarly, you must take time out to reflect on the words of scriptures, the teachings of your Guru and understand things logically. You will not be able to take your mind away from this world simply because your Guru tells you to do so. This is something that you have to learn to do, for your mind will not leave the world that easily.

The Importance of Reflection

You must deeply understand the nature of this world and why it is that the so-called happiness you experience is only an illusion. To do this, you will have to reduce the speed at which you are running towards the world so that you can reflect on where you should be attached. Avoid thinking about this world and gradually you will become neutral towards it. But your mind cannot remain without thinking. You have ordered it to withdraw from this world and it has obeyed you. But where should it go now? It cannot remain in a state of pause. It has to go somewhere or the other. And because of old, ingrained practices and the affinity for this world, its natural flow is towards the world, unless you show it some other place. The mind is a servant, and therefore it has no objection about where it goes. You have to repeatedly reflect on birth, death, old age and disease, reminding yourself that this world is not yours and that the spiritual happiness you seek is not here.

Your hunger will go on increasing here and will never be satiated, and you must constantly reflect on these truths. Reflection is the most important action in life, as it is this that will produce results. Why do you achieve success at one place and failure at another? It depends entirely on your thinking. Your past was determined by your thinking and your future will be too. Always remember this principle.

विषयान् ध्यायतश्चित्तं विषयेषु विषज्जते।
मामनुस्मरतश्चित्तं मय्येव प्रविलीयते॥ (*Bhagavatam* 11.14.27)

Veda Vyasa describes this beautifully in two lines: 'If you think about *mayic* objects, you will get attached to them. If you think about Me, you will get attached to Me.'

Everything depends on what you think. In twenty-four hours, how much time do you give to thinking that God is yours, and how much do you give to thinking that the world is yours? That's it! This is the yardstick. Now introspect. If you think God is mine for just two or four hours, then you will be benefitted accordingly. And when you continuously think, He alone is mine, then you will attain your goal. In the *Gita*, many verses emphasise the constant remembrance of God.

तेषां नित्याभियुक्तानां। (*Gita* 9.22)
यो मां स्मरति नित्यश:। (*Gita* 8.14)
सततं कीर्तयन्तो मां यतन्तश्च दृढव्रता:। (*Gita* 9.14)
एवं सततयुक्ता ये। (*Gita* 12.1)

The more you think, the quicker you will reach your goal. If you follow this then nothing else is required, neither the scriptures nor the *Vedas*.

Proper Guidance

नानुध्यायाद् बहूञ्छब्दान् वाचो विग्लापन॒ हि तत्॥

(Brihadaranyaka Upanishad 4.4.21)

This has been quoted by Jagadguru Shankaracharya. All the study of scriptures, all this knowledge is just a lot of mental gymnastics. Do not waste your time on it. That is why *surrendering* to the Guru has been advised. Understand from the Guru what is relevant and compulsory, leaving aside all irrelevant knowledge, and then constantly reflect on whatever you have learned.

विषया विनिवर्तन्ते निराहारस्य देहिन:।
रसवर्जं रसोऽप्यस्य परं दृष्ट्वा निवर्तते॥ *(Gita* 2.59)

There is a verse in the *Gita* which says that if someone renounces eating and drinking, then the objects of the senses cease to exist for him. If the objects of the senses cease, then it means that he has become liberated. If this is so, then what is the need for *bhakti*? Just go without food.

युक्ताहारविहारस्य युक्तचेष्टस्य कर्मसु।
युक्तस्वप्नावबोधस्य योगो भवति दु:खहा॥ *(Gita* 6.17)

But the *Gita* also says, 'Eating, sleeping, drinking and all our daily activities must be done properly and in moderation – not too much and not too little.' If you do not consume the right amount of proteins and vitamins, you will be punished by nature in the form of various diseases and afflictions. Consequently, you will be unable to progress materially or spiritually.

Food and Thoughts

The *Vedas* tell the story of Uddalaka Rishi, who advised his disciple, Shvetaketu, to eat and drink only *sattvic* items, because of the effect of food and drink on the mind. (We should not eat as the mind dictates — desserts of our choice or heavy, fried food. We have become slaves to the palate and get excited over different delicacies. All this has an indelible effect on the mind.)

Shvetaketu, however, could not understand the connection between food and the mind, because food is for the gross body, whereas the mind is subtle. 'What does a physical act like eating, whether a sweet or a dry piece of bread, have to do with the mind?' The food that we eat gets divided into three by-products: first is the excreta or waste, the second by-product is food turning into blood, flesh, bones, marrow and semen — all those things that constitute the physical body — and the third by-product is the nourishment and the development of the mind. In other words, our ideas are affected by what we eat and drink.

There are five sheaths or the *panchakosha* that cover the soul. Through your devotional practice, you can cross the first one, *annamaya*, and then food and drink will no longer affect you. Even consuming meat or alcohol will not affect your mind when you go beyond this level. But until you reach there, food will affect your mental state.

People ask me, 'Maharaj Ji, I cannot control my temper. I eat three to four chillies at a time.' I ask, 'Why do you eat so many chillies?' And they answer, 'I cannot eat food without them.' Then you are going to continue getting angry; you will have to bear the consequences. If you eat whimsically, you will reap the results.

In this way, Shvetaketu did not understand his Guru's instruction but was nevertheless bound by it. Noticing this, Uddalaka then ordered his disciple, 'No food for you today,' and he continued giving the same command for sixteen consecutive days. During his sixteen-day fast, Shvetaketu found it increasingly difficult to move about, and his head was spinning and he was dizzy. In this condition, his Guru asked him the pronunciation and meaning of some Vedic verses. Shvetaketu could not even open his eyes. On the seventeenth day, the Guru instructed that he be given some milk and then, a day or so later, some fruit juice. Now he asked him to recite a Vedic mantra, and he was able to recite the verse.

The Guru then asked him, 'My son, two days ago I asked you to recite these Vedic mantras and you were incapable of doing so. Now you can see the effect of food on the mind. *Sattvic* food creates a *sattvic* intellect, *rajasic* food, a *rajasic* intellect and *tamasic* food, a *tamasic* intellect. You should be very cautious about what you eat. You should not be a slave to your palate.'

रसवर्जं रसोऽप्यस्य परं दृष्ट्वा निवर्तते। (*Gita* 2.59)

There is another verse in the *Gita*: 'By renouncing food, the tendencies of the senses weaken and go away, but the tendencies of the mind, *vasanas*, or impressions of the subconscious coming from your past lives, will not leave you.'

Continuous fasting will only weaken the senses, which in turn will prevent them from working properly. Thus, the desires of the senses will end, but the desires of the mind will not. This *vasana* is the main thing.

All the scriptures declare the mind to be the main reason behind the human condition being bound by *maya*. Therefore, our mind must follow the instructions of the Guru and the scriptures. Our intellect is *mayic* and morally corrupt from many lifetimes of misuse. With this faulty intellect, we cannot determine what leads to our true well-being or causes our downfall. So, let your intellect be guided by the teachings of your Guru.

Using this purified intellect, you must govern your mind, and within a few days of practice, you will start accepting God as yours.

3

The Spiritual Hurdles

YOU HAVE BEEN TOLD so far that God is the soul of every soul and that every individual soul constitutes the body of God. Just as your material body constantly performs the service of its soul — from every thought to every action — at every moment, the body is trying to give happiness to the soul. In the same way, the individual soul is the eternal servant of God. Since beginningless time, however, we have run after objects of the world in order to gratify the senses, because we have considered the body to be the self. This sequence has taken place since time immemorial.

Nevertheless, if due to some good fortune any individual soul realises with full faith that its true nature is being an eternal servant of God, then there will be no delay in that soul attaining Him. In fact, there is no need for any other spiritual practice.

A question now arises in our mind: 'Who has to consider God as his? Who is supposed to love Him and *surrender* to Him?' These questions are important because the soul is a non-doer, and the work of the senses is not considered work even in the world, let alone in the realm of God. Even in a worldly court, if it is proven that a crime was accidental and that the accused had no intention of committing a crime, then he is not punished.

For example, if you are driving a car on the correct side of the road within the speed limit, and someone runs out from the other side of the road and lies down in front of your car, how can you be blamed for this death? 'He died under the wheels of my car, but I had no intention of killing him.' Similarly, consider if someone attacks you with a knife and you punch him in the stomach in self-defence, causing his death. You had no intention of killing him, but your punch ruptured a vital organ, and the result was fatal. This would not constitute murder, and you would not be considered an accused under Section 302 of the law.

Even a worldly government defines crime in terms of motive, which, of course, is applicable in the realm of God, too. The work of the senses is not noted there at all. If it were, we would have attained God, not just once but infinite times.

You have taken the name of God infinite times, fallen at the feet of Saints innumerable times and have seen countless descensions of God uncountable times. Having done all this should have enabled you to attain God by now and not just once but infinite times! However, you performed all this as a mere physical drill. You recited the names of God with your tongue, touched the feet of innumerable Saints and bowed your heads, but the inner machinery, the *antahkarana*, remained defective.

It is the mind that must be surrendered, that should realise, 'I am a servant of God.' The soul does not have to do this because the soul is a non-doer. If the soul had to do all this, then why would so many bad days befall us? It is true that the soul passes judgement on everything that is grasped by the senses.

For example, the eyes see something and pass it on to the mind, which likes it and sends it to the intellect, which, failing to decide on it, sends it back to the soul, which says, 'This is not mine.' Then the senses again do some work to present something else to the soul for its approval. In this way, you have spent infinite lifetimes in infinite universes seeing, smelling, tasting, hearing and feeling infinite things, and each time, the soul has passed its judgement: 'This is not mine.' Then what is yours? 'That I will not say, but when I get what is mine, I will say, "I have got it! I have got it! Stop! Stop! All my servants, the senses, mind and intellect, can now rest."' Until the soul obtains its subject – God – no servant can rest for a fraction of a second. As the *Gita* declares:

न हि कश्चित्क्षणमपि जातु तिष्ठत्यकर्मकृत्। (*Gita* 3.5)

They will have to serve the soul at every moment; they cannot resign or revolt. The doer, therefore, is the mind. The *antahkarana* is the inner machinery which has been defined earlier in great detail as consisting of the mind, plus the intellect and the ego or, simply, as the mind plus the intellect. Sometimes, it is just called the mind. The cause of your bondage and liberation, your pleasure and pain, your ultimate goal and the process to attain it is dependent entirely on the mind.

The Three Bodies

This mind is very intriguing. Until the bondage of the three types of bodies, *trisharira*, is crossed, this mind will not leave you. These three body types are the gross physical body, the subtle body and the causal body. When the soul crosses the bondage of these three, it becomes eternally blissful, liberated. Let us now understand these three bodies.

The Gross Body

This gross body is made of the five material elements and consists of the hands, feet, nose, ears, eyes, etc., and is made of flesh and bones, which you all can see before you. The five material elements – earth, water, fire, air and ether – comprise the gross body.

The Subtle Body

The subtle body is the most powerful of the three and comprises eighteen elements. Just look at this strange phenomenon: a subtle body comprises eighteen elements, while the gross body has only five. These eighteen elements comprise the five life airs (*prana*, *apana*, *udana*, *samana*, *vyana*), the five knowledge-acquiring senses (nose, eyes, tongue, skin and ears), the five working senses (hands, feet, tongue, and organs of reproduction and excretion), the mind, intellect and ego. You should know that this subtle body accompanies you after death, whether you go into the body of a cat or a dog or become the king of celestials, Indra. Wherever you go, this subtle body of eighteen elements will remain bound to the soul until you transcend the subtle body. On the path of *jnana*, this body can be destroyed, and on the path of *bhakti*, it can be made divine, but otherwise, this body will not leave you even at death. Sometimes when you are extremely troubled, you say, 'If I die, I would be free from all this.' But you will not be free because the cause of your problems is the subtle body, and this will accompany you after death. The physical body is not troubling you. Worry, happiness and distress are felt from within, by the mind. If you leave the gross body, what will happen? You will just get another one and the same problems will plague you, because the subtle body inside this one – your mind, intellect, knowledge-acquiring senses, and so on – will all remain the same and accompany you even after death.

The Causal Body

Beyond this subtle body is the causal body. This is very difficult to explain, but broadly speaking, it can be described as the body which is the seat of all your passions and desires. For instance, a seed contains within it the potential leaves, flowers, fruits, branches, etc. Now this may seem impossible on seeing the tiny seed, and you may even brush it aside as a joke, but bury that seed in the earth and see. Huge trees emerge from seeds. This is not the work of the earth; the earth is just the helper. The main force lies within the seed. In the same way, the causal body is shaped by the impressions of countless past lives and is the result of all the passions and desires arising from them. Thus, these three bodies are causing us trouble needlessly. It is when we cross these three that we are free from bondage.

However, there is another great danger – the pleasure of the *anandamaya kosha*. You have not yet received this. It is a very high level of pleasure. When you receive it, you have to be extremely cautious; otherwise, you stop at this point, believing it to be the highest state. It is, therefore, necessary to transcend the five kinds of sheaths – the *panchakosha* – to attain divine bliss.

The Five Veils

There are five sheaths, which are known as the *panchakosha*. The first is the *annamaya kosha*, or the food sheath. When you cross it, you come to the *pranamaya kosha* or the vital air sheath, then the *manomaya kosha* or the mental sheath, followed by the *vijnanamaya kosha* or the intellectual sheath, and finally the *anandamaya kosha* or the blissful sheath. It is only upon crossing all five sheaths that you attain ultimate bliss. Right now, you are wandering in the first *kosha*, the *annamaya*.

Annamaya Kosha

The gross body comprises the first sheath, *annamaya kosha*. The *anna* or food that you eat makes this body work. If you stop eating, the body stops working. It works properly only if given the right nourishment. If it is denied anything vital, it starts protesting and demanding food. If you ignore it, you will become sick, and if you do not give it anything, it will die. This is only natural, and the very reason why I mentioned earlier that food has a direct effect on the mind. Until you cross the level of the *annamaya kosha*, you will have to be careful with what you eat and drink because it will affect your mind. You have to avoid *tamasic* and *rajasic* foods, that is, hot, spicy and oily foods, because the mind becomes *rajasic* and *tamasic*, and the consequent bad effects will impede your devotional practice.

Pranamaya Kosha

The next sheath is the *pranamaya kosha*, consisting of the five life airs and the five working senses.

Manomaya Kosha

This sheath is made of a mixture of the five knowledge-acquiring senses and the mind.

Vijnanamaya Kosha

This sheath comprises the five knowledge-acquiring senses and the intellect.

Anandamaya Kosha

This is the most subtle sheath. You get some idea of this in deep sleep, when you do not experience the working of the senses, mind or intellect. You can understand this as the state of the causal body. Now if you cross this sheath, then the pleasure you experience is beyond the *annamaya kosha*. You get a glimpse of this every day, too, not in deep sleep, but when you are just entering into sleep from your waking state.

The Highest Worldly Pleasure

Everyone has their own style of sleeping, but when you put your head on the pillow and place your arms and legs naturally, the final moment before you cross over into sleep is but a glimpse of the *turiya* stage. This is the highest pleasure in the material world, while the second highest is in the state of dreamless, deep sleep. The third level of pleasure is derived from relationships and enjoyments from husband, wife, son, sweets, and so on.

Thus, the highest pleasures come free even to a poor man. He works hard all day and sleeps soundly at night without any dreams to disturb him. And the more affluent the man, the harder it is for him to get to sleep. He tosses and turns and dreams of being beaten, shouting and screaming, and so on. In other words, his troubles persist in his sleep. When such a person does not receive any pleasure during sleep, what can they expect to get in their waking state?

Dreams are experienced by everyone, more or less, but the average person who does his own work will enjoy a deeper sleep with fewer dreams. Everyone has dreams, but the number of dreams varies. Those of you who work hard sleep soundly at night, and those who do little during the day have dreams all night. Everyone has their own (karmic) accounts and receives pleasure and pain according to their individual destiny.

Whatever pleasure you may experience from the luxuries of this world is therefore surpassed by the pleasure of the *sushupti*, or deep sleep, and even greater than that is the moment of transition from a waking to a sleeping state. But all these are included in *anandamaya kosha*, and so it is only when you cross this sheath that you attain true bliss. This sheath, therefore, comes to an end only upon the attainment of God. The path of *jnana* consists of various spiritual disciplines to bring an end to these sheaths, but on the path of *bhakti*, an aspiring devotee does not have to do anything separately for this.

When a person eats, it is to satisfy his hunger with no knowledge of what will happen thereafter, but automatically, the food turns into fluid, then blood, flesh, fat, bones, marrow and semen. All these things are produced without any conscious effort on our part. We do not have the time to reflect on all of this, but we use them all. The body grows taller with the elongation of bones, and flesh is added to it. All of this happens without our knowing or being aware of it. Similarly, the fire of separation from God burns the five sheaths and the devotee has to make no separate endeavour to destroy them. There is no separate effort required on the path of devotion. So says the *Bhagavatam*:

अनिमित्ता भागवती भक्तिः सिद्धेर्गरीयसी।
जरयत्याशु या कोशं निगीर्णमनलो यथा। (*Bhagavatam* 3.25.33)

The Critical Point

The point I am making you understand is that the ultimate bliss you seek is beyond even the *anandamaya kosha*. When you cross the *vijnanamaya kosha* and reach the *anandamaya kosha*, you will experience great pleasure. This, however, is the ultimate point of danger. If your Guru has not attained perfection, that is, he has not attained God, then you will stop here, thinking, 'What greater pleasure than this could there possibly be?' For example, if you place some candy along with some diamonds and pearls and other various valuables before a little child, he will select the candy, according to his level of understanding.

When the soul, hungry for pleasure since eternity, finally crosses the *vijnanamaya kosha* and experiences the great pleasure of the *anandamaya kosha*, he will need a guardian to warn him, 'Do not stop here! This is the final point of danger.' If the Guru is not there at that time, then the spiritual aspirant can be in a precarious position.

The Enemy of God

This mind, which is so extraordinary, must therefore be surrendered. It is the mind that must think God is mine and reflect on what is preventing this from happening, which, as I am pointing out to you repeatedly, is the ego. The degree to which the ego is present in you is the degree to which you are troubled. There are devotional songs being sung here[1] that are full of divine bliss, the content of which you will only be able to appreciate fully after you attain God. Some people do try to enjoy the sweetness inherent in these songs by reflecting on the sentiments, but others have fallen into the habit of just singing verbally as though they are drinking bitter medicine, instead of trying to evoke sentiment according to the spirit of the song. You will have to work very hard and make a more determined effort.

The obstacle creating disturbance in your *sadhana* is the ego. There is one enemy of God and that is ego, even though God Himself says in the *Gita*, 'I have no enemy, nor do I have any friend.'

समोऽहं सर्वभूतेषु न मे द्वेष्योऽस्ति न प्रिय:। (*Gita* 9.29)

This is said just to fool you! God does, in fact, have a friend – humility, the opposite of pride. God comes within your grasp through humility, but even after He has entered your heart, He will run away if He sees pride. Indeed, there is great enmity between these two, just as darkness and light are opposed to each other and cannot reside together in one place.

ईश्वरस्याप्यभिमानद्वेषित्वाद् दैन्यप्रियत्वाच्च ॥

(Narada Bhakti Sutra 27)

Sage Narada, in his *Bhakti Sutra*, therefore says that God has an aversion to pride and that He loves humility. Pride is such an enemy of His that no matter how great the personality, He grants no concessions.

An Encounter with Pride

Once in Dvarika, Shri Krishna's wife Rukmini, His personal weapon, Sudarshana Chakra,[2] and His divine mount, Garuda, all developed pride. Shri Krishna thought, 'I have to teach them a lesson, but they are not going to pay heed to any lecture. I have to think of something else.'

Being *liladhari*, He was forever manifesting new pastimes. He summoned Garuda and said, 'Fetch me a flower from the pond of Kuber. I have heard that the fragrance of these celestial flowers is exquisite.' This was not a difficult task for Garuda. 'As You order, my Lord.' Garuda, having access to the three worlds could reach anywhere in the universe without effort or strain of any sort. He immediately flew to Kuber's lake in the celestial abodes and started plucking a lotus blooming in the pond. As he was about to pluck it, Hanumana, the great devotee of Shri Rama, who was now old and happened to be sitting there, drowsily asked him, 'Who are you and why are you plucking that flower?' Garuda answered, 'I am Garuda and I am taking this flower for Shri Krishna.' Hanumana said, 'How dare you pluck this flower without permission!' Garuda replied, 'Permission? Whose permission do I need?' On hearing this, Hanumana took two steps forward, grabbed Garuda and held him under his armpit. Garuda tried his best to free himself from Hanumana's grip, but to no avail. Hanumana then plucked the flower and went with great speed to Dvarika, thinking, 'Let me see my Beloved Lord on this pretext.'

As he came close to Dvarika, Sudarshana Chakra, which always circled Dvarika, guarding it, stopped him, as it was its duty to protect Dvarika from enemies. The Chakra cuts to pieces any enemy that tries to enter Dvarika. When Sudarshana Chakra saw this majestic but fearsome form travelling at great speed towards Dvarika, it confronted him. But Hanumana caught it and put it under his other armpit and walked gallantly straight into Shri Krishna's palace without bothering to ask for permission! Which gatekeeper is going to stand up to someone who can trap Garuda and the Chakra in his armpits?

Now, before he arrived, Shri Krishna told Rukmini, 'Hanumana is coming with great speed and he seems angry.' She asked, 'Why?' He answered, 'Don't ask why right now; we have to hurry.' She said, 'And do what?' Shri Krishna proposed, 'I will become Rama and you become Sita, or else he will devastate your Dvarika in a second.'

Shri Krishna became Rama instantly out of fear, but who could become Sita? Rukmini did not have the courage, so Shri Krishna advised Rukmini, 'Pray to Shri Radha. She will come immediately and become Sita. Otherwise, Dvarika will be destroyed. Neither you nor I will survive.'

Rukmini meditated on Shri Radha, 'O Maharani, have mercy on us. We are all in danger.' Kishori Ji took the form of Devi Sita and arrived. Hanumana arrived soon after in an angry mood but found his beloved Sita and Rama seated there.

Shri Krishna questioned him, 'What do you have under both armpits?' 'I was in the garden of Kuber, and this bird [Garuda] came and was speaking nonsense and misbehaving, so I put him under my armpit.' 'And in the other armpit?' 'There was some shiny object spinning around your city like a top [Sudarshana Chakra], so I caught it and put it in my other armpit.' Shri Krishna said, 'What will you do with this bird and of what use will this toy be to you? Leave them.' Hanumana released them.

In this way, the pride of Rukmini, Garuda and Sudarshana Chakra was decimated. Thus, Shri Krishna enacted this divine *lila* to reveal the fact that He spares no one, not even His friends or wives, not even someone playing the role of His father.

Arjuna's Humbling Experience

Similarly, Arjuna once developed pride, believing himself to be special. 'Shri Krishna cleans and bathes my horses and tends to them after battle. He drives my chariot and respects me so much that He gave me His sister in marriage and made me His brother-in-law.' First of all, Arjuna had the reputation of being the wielder of the famous Gandiv bow, and on top of that, he received so much affection and respect from Shri Krishna that he became proud. Shri Krishna thought, 'This is an unnecessary disease that he has developed and requires an immediate cure, because this is a danger which may escalate later.'

One day, when they were roaming in the forest, they came upon a man wielding a sword in his left hand and eating fallen, dried leaves with his right one. Arjuna told Shri Krishna, 'This man appears to be mad, eating dried leaves.' Shri Krishna said, 'He must be a drunkard.' Arjuna went to him and inquired, 'Why are you eating dry leaves?' The man replied, 'Do not disturb me unnecessarily. It is none of your business. Go on your way.' Arjuna suggested, 'But there are so many green leaves around.' Annoyed, the man replied, 'Don't prattle uselessly! For this contemptible stomach, why should I pull living leaves off a living tree? How would you like it if I pulled the hair off your head?' Arjuna thought to himself, 'These are not the words of a drunkard, but even a crackpot can sometimes say something wise.'

He further asked, 'Why are you carrying a sword in your left hand?' The old man said, 'Do not waste my time with all this talk and do not be an impediment in my work.' Nevertheless, Arjuna persisted, 'What is the secret behind this? It does not befit a *baba* to wield a sword so carefully in his left hand. Please tell me.' The old man asked, 'What do you do?' Arjuna answered, 'I am an expert with the bow and arrow.' The old man prompted, 'Then can you do me a favour and kill three people?' Arjuna said, 'I can kill millions in seconds!' The old man said, 'Then the first person is Bhrigu Rishi.' Arjuna was startled. Such a great soul as Bhrigu, and this stranger was talking about killing him! Why? 'My Krishna was resting and without any reason, Bhrigu came and kicked Him in the chest.' Arjuna said, 'This is not possible. He is a Brahmin, and I am a Kshatriya. How could I possibly kill a Brahmin?'

'Then why are you talking uselessly and claiming that you can do anything? The second person is a woman – Draupadi. She fed the remnants of herself and her husband to my beloved Krishna.' Arjuna thought, 'How do I tell him that she is my wife?' So he said, 'Killing a woman is not appropriate for a valiant warrior; he will be defamed in history. People would say, "This is the famous wielder of the Gandiv bow, and he could not find someone other than a woman to kill." I cannot release an arrow on a woman.'

'Well, there is one person left. Will you be able to kill him?' Arjuna asked, 'Is it a Brahmin or a woman?' The old man said, 'No.' Arjuna spoke, 'Then who is it?' The old man replied, 'Arjuna.' Arjuna thought, 'He wants to use me to kill myself? If I tell him that I am Arjuna, he might finish me off.' Who knows what power he has? He seems to be an extraordinary personality, and nothing is impossible for ascetics and sages.

Arjuna then asked, 'What has Arjuna done to displease you?' The old man answered, 'He used Krishna to take care of his horses and had various menial tasks done by Him. I am extremely angry with him.' Arjuna said, 'I will take your leave now.' It seemed best to him to run, given the fact that he was Arjuna. He would not be able to find Bhrigu or Draupadi, but he was there, and Shri Krishna could not be trusted! 'Shri Krishna might reveal my identity. He just likes to play around and watch what happens.'

Arjuna ran back and told Shri Krishna, 'We ought to return. I think we have travelled a little too far.' Shri Krishna asked, 'What happened?' Arjuna said, 'I will tell you later. First, let's get out of here.'

Pride is therefore intolerable in anyone for God, and He spares no one, let alone His loved ones. A mother will give money to a doctor to have her son's boil surgically removed. But if the neighbour's son has one, she just offers her opinion to the neighbour: 'Have it operated on or it will cause harm.' She does not care whether he follows through with the advice. How does it concern her? Those who are His, those who are in the process of surrendering to Him and those who are surrendered are especially the object of His concern.

In this way, humility is most dear to God while pride is His greatest enemy. We should understand this and always be vigilant to protect ourselves from pride and constantly move towards humility.

4

The Path of Surrender

THE PATHS OF *KARMA*, *jnana* and *bhakti* are extremely difficult to follow in order to attain the grace of God. According to the *Vedas*, each one of the rules and regulations must be followed on the path of *karma*, and in this Kaliyuga, not a single one can be followed. The path of *jnana* is even more difficult, and so is *bhakti*. There is a fourth route available, which is described towards the end of the *Gita* as the most confidential subject.

सर्वगुह्यतमं भूय: शृणु मे परमं वच:।
इष्टोऽसि मे दृढमिति ततो वक्ष्यामि ते हितम्॥ (Gita 18.64)

The Lord says, 'Arjuna, I have spoken on many confidential subjects — *karma*, *jnana* and *bhakti*.' But Arjuna had still not reached the point where he was ready to fight the Mahabharata War and kill the enemy as per Shri Krishna's instruction. Arjuna still did not have the courage to carry this out and to confide his inability to do so to Shri Krishna, so He said, 'Listen, since you are very dear to Me, I will tell you about the most confidential of all subjects.'

56

सर्वधर्मान्परित्यज्य मामेकं शरणं व्रज।
अहं त्वां सर्वपापेभ्यो मोक्षयिष्यामि मा शुच:॥ (*Gita* 18.66)

This verse of the *Gita* states, 'Come into My shelter.'

This essentially means 'surrender to Me'. This is the most important and an unfailing remedy for all souls, because there would be just a tiny handful of souls who, due to their previous good *sanskaras*, would be *karmi*, *jnani* or *yogi*. But this is not a general rule, and I am not ready to accept that out of six billion people,[1] there would be even six who are proper *karmis*, proper *jnanis* or proper *bhaktas*. Such people are very, very rarely found. For the general *sadhaka*, the simplest path is usually the most beneficial. Anything too complicated or difficult has associated risks. If there is a crooked or thorny path that goes between rivers and canals, it is all right if someone wants to take that path to show that he is brave by accepting it. But why should we take such a risk when we have the safest and surest path? The path of surrender.

The *Gita* (18.66) states, 'Resign all your duties to Me, take refuge in Me alone and I shall free you from all sins; worry not.'

Surrender provides such a big entitlement. All other relationships — father, mother, brother, son or any other relation — take second place to the surrendered soul for a Saint or God. All other relationships come to an end. I will now tell you about a historical incident that illustrates this point.

The Divine Privilege of Surrender

Sage Galava and Chitrasena

There was a sage by the name of Galava, who had attained various perfections. He was making offerings to the sun when a Gandharva called Chitrasena, who was travelling in the sky, accidentally spat into the water Galava was offering. Galava became enraged and immediately went to Shri Krishna, 'The gods that You appoint are so insolent! Look at what Chitrasena has just done.' Seeing his anger, Shri Krishna pacified him, 'He has indeed made a grave mistake. I vow to kill him within twenty-four hours.' Look at the harsh punishment for something that was done unintentionally, just because it involved Sage Galava! Meanwhile, when Sage Narada came to know about this, he felt it was inappropriate and that the guiltless Chitrasena was being punished unnecessarily. He also knew, however, that he could not sort things out between Galava and Shri Krishna, because Galava was insistent on the punishment and Shri Krishna had already taken a vow to give it. So Sage Narada went to Chitrasena, who begged him for protection. The former said, 'All right, I will do something.' But what? To speak to Shri Krishna after He had already taken a vow was useless, and if he annoyed Galava and got cursed by him, then there would not be left even a trace of ashes of Sage Narada.

So Sage Narada went to Subhadra, Shri Krishna's sister and Arjuna's wife, and said, 'Today and tomorrow are days of special significance. When you bathe in the Yamuna River tomorrow, if someone asks you for anything and you give it, you will reap an imperishable reward for it.' Setting her up in this manner, Sage Narada then went to Chitrasena and said, 'Tomorrow, go to the banks of Yamuna River and sob piteously. If a woman approaches you and asks, "What trouble are you in?", tell her to first vow to help you, and only then tell her about your problem. When she has given her vow, tell her that Shri Krishna has vowed to kill you, and your work will be done.'

Chitrasena did as he was told and received a vow of protection from her because he had surrendered to her. Chitrasena then said, 'Your brother has vowed to kill me.' Subhadra replied, 'Today, I will have to give you more importance than my brother because you have taken shelter with me. I must fulfil the conditions you ask.' Saying thus, she went to Arjuna. 'As my husband, you have to protect my vow made to a surrendered soul.' Arjuna declared, 'Today, no one is my friend or Lord, nor am I anyone's servant. I will protect Chitrasena from Shri Krishna.'

Now the stage was set for a 'mahabharata' right there at home. Who is going to explain to whom when such big personalities are involved? Shri Krishna raised His Chakra and warned Arjuna, 'Go back home. Your Gandiv bow will not work here. I have taken a vow to sever his head.' Arjuna replied, 'I have a weapon that equals Your Chakra that I did not use during the Mahabharata, the Pashupat Astra.[2] I am releasing it, so be warned.' Both these weapons were unfailing, and if released together, the entire universe, aside from Arjuna and Shri Krishna, would be obliterated. Having recited their respective invocations, Shri Krishna and Arjuna released their weapons, and the whole world was in an uproar.

Lord Shiva left His abode and His *samadhi* and stood between their weapons. 'What are you both doing?' Both weapons were intent on cutting off the head of the opposing party. Lord Shiva folded his hands and entreated them, 'Try and remember the purpose for which this world was created, and act according to that purpose. This will cause total annihilation of everyone except Arjuna and Shri Krishna, and what will be the benefit?' In this way, He pacified both, and Chitrasena was saved.

But now Galava's purpose had been tampered with, and he was furious. He said, 'They have all united together – brother, sister and brother-in-law – and Chitrasena has not been punished. I will destroy all four.' He lifted some water in his hands and started invoking a mantra. Arjuna looked at Subhadra. Subhadra lifted some water herself and, using the supreme power of her devotion, she nullified the power of Galava's asceticism, and the water did not fall from Galava's hand. What I am trying to point out by saying all this is that surrender is such a big thing that it nullifies all other relationships, whether its your father, brother or sister. It occupies the supreme place in the heart of God and His devotees, the Saints.

Surrender and Faith

God, therefore, says that surrender is the most confidential knowledge. As the *Gita* states,

सर्वगुह्यतमं भूयः शृणु मे परमं वचः।
इष्टोऽसि मे दृढमिति ततो वक्ष्यामि ते हितम्॥ (*Gita* 18.64)

Hear again, My supreme instruction, the most confidential of all. Because you are very dear to Me, I am speaking this for your benefit.

But you have not been able to achieve this surrender since eternity. You therefore do not have faith either in God or in the Guru. The *Vedas* declare:

यस्य देवे परा भक्तिर्यथा देवे तथा गुरौ।

(*Shvetashvatara Upanishad* 6.23)

You must have the same sentiment and the same level of devotion towards both. But we do not do this because of a lack of desire to surrender, a lack of faith. What is faith? Where there is faith, there is favourable thinking always. That is the definition – to always think favourably. Is a woman faithful to her husband? If she is, she would be equally happy to eat whatever her husband puts on her plate – whether it was delectable or detestable. Is there any such woman? No. Then there is no wife who is faithful. The vow of faithfulness is fidelity, whether to father, mother, Guru or God. It means to keep your desires in line with theirs, to not apply your own logic to their actions and to always think favourably. This constitutes surrender.

The story of Tukarama is a case in point. He retained full confidence in the actions of God even during the loss of his wealth, the death of his wife and the death of his son.

On the other hand, someone who is foolish, who has not surrendered, would immediately start questioning, 'I went to the temple for *sankirtana* and a robbery took place at my home! What did your God do? What kind of protection does your Guru provide?' But it is only your welfare that is the reason behind all this. The various means and methods utilised for your well-being are known only to God and the Guru. How can you possibly understand? If your intellect could understand the secret that behind every action is your well-being, then there would be no difference between you, the Guru and God. You could all then don the robes of a spiritual master.

Thus, faith is achieved only through detachment from the world. The scriptures state that faith must come first; otherwise, you may listen to infinite lectures, meet infinite Saints or descensions of God, but you will not progress. Nothing is achievable without faith.

Only the person who is inclined to think favourably – that is, only the one who has faith – will be successful on the path of surrender. But the one who constantly uses his intellect, questions everything or must understand everything before accepting anything will not be able to surrender or receive God's grace in infinite lifetimes. The intellect is material and therefore will not be able to grasp things at first. Even in the world we accept things first and understand them later. 'This is your mother and this is your father.' Okay, but what is the meaning of mother and father? You will understand this much later.

Similarly, you use radios and other devices, don't you? Yes. Do you understand the technicalities of how a radio transmits a voice or how any device works? No. You are just concerned with using it. We therefore accept that things work in a particular way, and we use them. If you want to understand how, then you can study and acquire that knowledge over time. If you say that you want the knowledge first before using something, then that is utterly impossible.

In the spiritual field, too, one must first do devotional practice. After this comes practical experience, and only then does one develop complete knowledge. First, you must accept the theory; otherwise, how will you begin your practice?

For example, in school, you are told about a line. It is defined as that which has length, but no breadth. But whatever you draw has some breadth, has some thickness to it, doesn't it? Yes, but to explain it, all this has to be done. A teacher asks a boy to subtract five from five. The child does not answer. 'Why haven't you answered?' The boy says, 'Because the answer is nothing.' The teacher counters, 'Why didn't you write a zero then?' The child answers, 'Because zero means nothing, so I wrote nothing.' The teacher emphasises, 'No, no. It is compulsory that you write zero. You must comply with this, even if you don't understand.'

Those of you who studied algebra will be familiar with this. Let us say Ramesh's age equals 'a'. You work on the problem, and the actual age represented by 'a' is revealed. This shows that you do these various tasks based on faith, and as you are taught how to solve the problems, you understand why this is being done.

Despite this, we go ahead and apply our intellect immediately in the area of God, when there is so little we understand, even in this *mayic* realm. People do not understand their wives, husbands or sons. 'After all these years, my eyes have finally opened, and I realise what kind of person he is.' This means that you did not understand beforehand, and what you understand now is also limited, as there is so much more that you will understand in the future. All your understanding right now is imperfect; it is all faulty. The path of surrender is therefore topmost and is the method by which we can attain God's grace.

Humility

The most important thing to do to surrender to God is to become humble, to become devoid of pride.

Gauranga Mahaprabhu says in his *Shikshashtaka* that if you want to receive the grace of God, you must be humbler than a blade of grass. What do you have that you should be proud? Why do you think of yourself as special? What are you? And what will you become after death? A cat, a dog, a tree or an insect? A tree was asked, 'Were you not a professor in your last life, with a doctorate in literature? You were told to go and seek the shelter of God, to humble yourself. But at that time, you said, "I am a PhD, I do not blindly follow anything." Now look at your condition. At that time, because of your educational qualifications or something else, you could not humble yourself before God.' In this way, without humility, there is no scope for even beginning your spiritual practice.

Shelter of Shoes

There was a Saint called Venkatanatha. When he started on the path of God, he met tremendous opposition. This happens to all Saints. His opponents decided to hang a garland of shoes across his doorway. As he was always blissfully unaware of what was happening around him, they hoped he would walk through his doorway and knock the shoes, and they would all get to laugh and ridicule him. When Venkatanatha came walking in his own natural style and the shoes hit him on the head, he started laughing. Instead of showing anger and abuse towards his tormentors, he manifested humility and surprised his opponents. He said, 'Some people take the shelter of the path of *karma* and some the path of *jnana*, but I have attained God by taking the shelter of His servants' shoes.' Whosoever has a longing to see God must practise and manifest humility.

Laugh It Off

You must have heard of a great philosopher called Socrates. He had an ill-tempered wife for whom abuse was an everyday affair. I am not saying that all wives are like her. Socrates knew that it was just the play of the three *gunas* within her that caused her to be troubled in this way, so he would shrug off her outbursts by laughing. Once, not being able to incite him to anger, she poured a bucket of water over him. Socrates turned to his friend and said, 'You know there is always a shower after a thunderstorm,' and laughed. His friend remarked, 'How can you take this kind of misbehaviour from your wife?' Socrates replied, 'We are not really fighting, but putting on a performance for you to watch. As husband and wife, we joke and play around like this all the time.' In this way, Socrates would turn any sort of provocation into a joke and laugh it off. What is the benefit from responding to it anyway? The ability to do this comes with humility.

Just Ash!

There was a Muslim Saint called Usman who was walking with his disciples when someone happened to throw a basket of ash from an upper floor window that accidentally fell on him. When Usman was covered in ashes, he looked up and said, 'O God! You are very merciful.' When his friend asked him the reason for saying this, he said, 'It would have been appropriate if burning coals were thrown all over me, for I love this world instead of God. He, being so merciful, has only thrown these ashes on me.' Instead of retaliating in anger, Usman responded with humility.

We must become this humble. Our condition right now, however, is that even if someone tells us something true about ourselves, we cannot control our anger. This is true even of those who have taken the renounced order of *samnyasa*, let alone common householders. Humility is therefore paramount.

Without humility, your spiritual life cannot start, and there is no other way.

5

The Nature of Love

THERE ARE THREE THINGS to be understood: *premi* – the lover; *premaspada* – the beloved; and *prema* – divine love. Love in this context implies the intimate meeting of the lover and the beloved, that is, their internal attachment. In other words, love unites the lover and the beloved. The lover is the one who loves, the beloved is the object of love and divine love is the binding force between the lover and the beloved.

You might think that you already know all this and that you have put it into practice since eternity with your mother, father, son, wife, and so on. However, the fact is that you have neither known nor accepted what love is, and you have never put it into practice. Thinking you have is merely your own delusion. There is no lover or beloved in this world and neither is possible as long as you remain under the influence of *maya*, even if you have endeavoured to find them over infinite lifetimes. The reason is that the definition of 'beloved' is so demanding that it applies to no one, and therefore no one can become a lover or acquire love.

Premaspada (beloved) implies the treasure house of love, and the person begging from the treasurer is called a *premi*

67

(lover). Love is beyond the grasp of any person under *maya*, even Indra, the king of celestials. When no one in the *mayic* realm can fulfil the role of the beloved, then how can anyone become a lover? And if someone were to become a lover, without a genuine beloved, what would he gain?

You can acquire wealth in the world only by surrendering to a wealthy person and wisdom only by surrendering to a wise person. A person can only give you what he or she possesses. But if someone has no wealth to begin with, what can he give to the one who surrenders to him, even if he says, 'Here, take whatever I have'? People can claim that they will help all they like, but all that worldly people possess is begging bowls, that too, broken ones. In other words, what can they give you when they do not have what you want? All worldly people are devoid of love, being beggars themselves, whether they are Indra, Kubera, Varuna, Yamaraja or ordinary human beings. Someone may possess extraordinary powers, but he does not possess love and it is love that you desire. It is love that your soul is yearning for. From where will they get it to give it to you, even if they desire to do so?

When it comes to deception, it is prevalent throughout the entire world. Everyone wants to lay claim to being a beloved. Whether it is the relationship between mother and son, husband and wife or others, everyone is bent on controlling the other by assuming the position of a beloved without having the corresponding love within. A person who is devoid of love cannot assume the position of the beloved. How does one become a lover, and what will you gain by doing so?

We have taken infinite births in the form of the 8.4 million species of life since eternity looking for just one thing – love. We have begged for it from our mothers, fathers, husbands, wives and children. And everyone has said, 'Here, take it! I have a storehouse of love for you.' But no one even knows the true definition of love, let alone possesses it.

Bestower of Love

Love is only in the possession of God-realised Saints who have received this power from a genuine lover. From where is this love acquired? God does not bestow it directly. It is beyond Shri Radha–Krishna's capability to do so, even though They are *premaspada*, the reservoir of love. It is distributed by Their lovers, the Saints. Shri Radha–Krishna are the treasury, the abode of love, but They do not bestow love directly. They instead give it through Their lovers. No soul can have direct contact with Shri Radha–Krishna at any time. Only a Rasika Saint who has attained divine love can grace a surrendered soul with divine love. This soul thereby gives love to others who surrender to him. Thus, divine love is bestowed in this manner.

You all know the story of Uddhava, the intimate friend of Shri Krishna. Shri Krishna did not bless Uddhava with divine love because it was beyond His authority to do so. He was, however, concerned about how to bless His friend with it. The ultimate authorities of divine love were the *gopis* and so Shri Krishna sent Uddhava to them. Uddhava accepted them as his Guru – not through some process of receiving a mantra whispered in his ear – but through complete surrender. After complete purification from within, the disciple surrenders to the Guru who has attained divine love and ultimately receives it from him. Both these conditions must be completely fulfilled.

Guru Mantra

One who proclaims himself as a Guru without having attained divine love is a fraud. Unfortunately, in our country nowadays, you can see pseudo babas deceiving gullible people by whispering some mantra into their ear, with no regard given to that person's eligibility. Even to enter a law school, it is compulsory for the student to have a graduate qualification. And yet for these imposters, everyone is a candidate for divine love! Anyone who comes to them is initiated as their disciple. What exactly is given? A mantra whispered in their ear. What happens after that?

The person is still under *maya*, so lust, anger, greed, envy, infatuation – all vices remain. Such a person has not attained infinite bliss, nor has he or she realised God. What type of initiation is this? He is a demon, and he has deceived you. What has he given to you by whispering something in your ear? During the construction of a new house, for example, a qualified electrician ensures that all the electrical fittings, such as lights, fans, and so on, are professionally installed before connecting the house to the main power supply. If all the various connections have been done correctly, then it is impossible for the lights and fans to not work. If this occurs, then it is likely that there is some problem at the power supplier's end. And if the power supply is flowing freely, why connect it to the house when it is still under construction and all the fittings are not yet installed or in place? Similarly, what is the need for a Guru who whispers a special mantra? There is no mantra greater than the name of God, nor can there ever be. This is my challenge. Let any Saint come forward and prove otherwise.

What name is being given to you in secret? If I say, 'O Rama, I offer my obeisance to You,' in Hindi, a teacher in one of these sects would say, 'No! No! Say *Om Rama Ramaya Namah* (in Sanskrit).' Does this dispute over language exist in the divine realm, too? Does God want to be addressed only in Sanskrit? And do you think He objects if you say the same thing in Bengali, Punjabi, Tamil, Telugu, English or any other language? 'This is not a mantra; this is not My name!' Look at the ignorance that exists!

The Eligibility

A lot of people claim that their Guru has descended from Goloka. All right, when he made you his disciple, what did he give you? A mantra. And what happened after that? Nothing. But there is a power that he is supposed to give you – divine love, which when enters inside you, you instantly attain God and become free from *maya* forever. Even if you accept your Guru to be greater than God, it would still amount to nothing. He will have to be a Saint who has attained divine love, and if he has, you will still have to be eligible to receive divine love, which means your heart must be completely pure for him to accept you as a disciple.

You must have heard that Jagadguru Shankaracharya and a few other Saints only made two or three disciples in their entire lifetimes and that too after rigorous testing and engaging them in intense spiritual practice. When their mind was completely pure, then their Guru gave them initiation or *diksha*. After that, there is nothing left to be done. The receptacle was prepared for what the Guru had to give. Just like when you build a house, you must ensure all electrical fittings are professionally installed before the electrician connects your house to the main power supply. Similarly, when the receptacle is ready, God bestows divine love through the Guru and not personally. It is not that He cannot do so, but He has laid down this eternal law and does not violate it. Even if someone challenges Him to do so, He will not break His law. Divine love can only be bestowed by a Saint.

Kinds of Saints

Thus, who is the treasure house of divine love, the *premaspada*? The Saint. Saints can be of many kinds. Let us understand three of them: the *jnani* Saint, the *yogi* Saint and the *bhakta* or devotee Saint. The *jnani* Saint cannot give you divine love; his grace extends only as far as granting liberation. He himself has not attained divine love. Neither can the *yogi* Saint. He can grant you various supernatural powers – *anima, laghima, garima,* etc. – which allow you to fly in the sky and assume a thousand bodies, and so on, but he cannot give you divine love.

Even great yogis and sages hanker for divine love. The foremost *jnanis* – Sanaka, Janaka, Shuka, for instance – went to Braja for the same bliss and assumed the form of trees, hoping that the *gopis* would bestow their grace upon them in the form of divine love. I am talking about liberated, perfectly pure *paramahamsas*, not those people who take *samnyasa* simply by wearing saffron robes and roam around. Divine love cannot be given either by the *yogi* Saint or the *jnani* Saint, but only by the devotee Saint and no one else, no other category of Saint – not even God. Then what can a poor worldly person give you? Such a person does not have even a trace of divine love. The treasure house of divine love is the devotee Saint and God. However, the devotee Saint has received it through another Saint. Divine love is Shri Krishna's personal power, His most private, personal power, and He remains under its control.

Enslave God

Divine love is a power of God, and yet God remains under its control. But He declares that He is supremely independent, who can control Him!

अहं भक्त पराधीनो ह्यस्वतन्त्र इव द्विज। (*Bhagavatam* 9.4.63)

I am subordinate to My devotees. They have taken away My independence and have enslaved Me.

Whosoever attains divine love can enslave God, be it an ignorant simpleton, a dog, a cat or even a crow like Kagabhushundi, the great Saint who had the body of a crow! Moreover, this enslavement is not for a day or two either, but for eternity. God is not performing any kind of forced labour, like a servant does in the world, who does it reluctantly because he needs the money and would joyfully give it up if he could get the money through some other means. People are so happy when they get a day off at work.

Maybe a renowned person has died, but they still receive their pay. You can imagine how happy they would be if they could get a lifetime's salary without doing any work. God, on the other hand, does not perform a service like this. How does He serve His devotee? He receives immense pleasure performing even the most menial task for His devotee. He does not do it reluctantly like worldly workers: 'Oh! Now that this soul has received divine love, I will have to serve him because I am under his control.' He is not under any such compulsion.

Causeless Mercy

He willingly distributes divine love among the souls. His most confidential power is *hladini shakti,* and the absolute essence of this is divine love. He irresistibly distributes this even to insignificant souls like us. Why? He cannot control Himself due to His innate nature of being infinitely compassionate. He causelessly graces everyone and never regrets this action.

It is not like the case with Lord Shiva and the demon Bhasmasura, where He gave the demon the boon that anyone on whose head he placed his hand would be destroyed. Bhasmasura immediately wanted to place his hand on Lord Shankara's head, and He was forced to escape to save Himself from the effects of His own boon, freely given. Finally, Shri Krishna had to come to His rescue by tricking the demon and making him place his hand on his own head.

Similarly, it is not that Shri Krishna regrets giving divine love to any soul because it would enslave Him, and He would have much rather stayed peacefully in Goloka. He performs menial tasks for His rustic, illiterate devotees, such as keeping guard at the door for one person, grinding flour for another and caring for the horses of another.

There are innumerable examples in our history, not just ten or twenty. He bestows His personal power on His child and becomes happy seeing His child in such ecstasy. Even worldly mothers sometimes sacrifice their food to feed their children. They willingly go hungry to feed their child properly. And if there is no more food left, they manage with whatever is available at home. Now because this is a worldly relationship based on selfishness, happiness isn't always involved. But by serving His devotees, God experiences bliss that is even greater than the ultimate bliss of divine love experienced by an individual soul.

The treasure house of divine love is therefore God and the Saint who has received it. The rest of the world, whether they be yogis, *jnanis*, sages, ascetics or spiritual aspirants, cannot be *premaspada*, because they do not possess divine love. No one can aspire to this position if he or she is under the influence of *maya*. It is utterly impossible!

You must have understood now who is to be loved — God and His associates, the Saints. That is all. Do not take your mind anywhere else, whether it is a celestial god or goddess, as they all are under *maya*. It is because of your devotion to them that countless lives have been wasted. Initially, people used to worship the celestials mentioned in the scriptures, but nowadays they are concocting other gods to worship. However, be it any celestial god or goddess, all are under *maya*. The only object of your love, whom you can call your *premaspada*, are God and His associates (Saints), because they possess divine love. The main reservoir is God, and the individual souls He gives divine love to are called devotees, His associates, the Saints. After God-realisation, only a Saint is authorised to bless you with divine love. However, God and the Saint are not two different personalities. When you practise devotion to the Guru, God is pleased, and when you practise devotion to God, the Guru is pleased. This is not a worldly relationship with worldly jealousies. God Himself has declared this at thousands of places in the scriptures.

मद्भक्तस्य ये भक्तास्ते मे भक्ततमा मता:॥ (Veda Vyasa)

Those who are devotees of My devotees, I consider them to have practised devotion to Me a thousandfold, and I shower My grace upon them correspondingly.

In other words, God is more pleased by devotion to His devotees than He is by devotion to Himself. This is the direct statement of God and so there is no conflict here. Nevertheless, divine love will be given only by the Guru. This is the law. If Shri Krishna decides to grace you, He will have divine love given to you through one of His Saints. And you do not have to look for them; they will find you. There are always one, two or more of His Saints in the world at any given time, particularly if there is great turmoil in the world. In Braja, 5,000 years ago, Saints descended in their droves; even the trees were Saints! There is always some Saint or the other in the world; it is never without them. If it were, then it would come to an end, for it is they who sustain the universe by their presence.

Conditions Apply

You must have now understood the meaning of the term *premaspada*, the object of love. Let us now understand *premi*, the lover. We must love, and you now know who is to be loved. I have also told you that love is a power of God that will be given to you by the Guru when you are eligible or worthy of receiving it. This love is not something you can practise, because your mind, intellect and senses are material, and the object of love is divine. It is impossible to practise love with the impure, *mayic* mind. Not difficult, impossible! When you receive the power of love from your Guru, only then can you say you love God, not before. To purify your mind and make it eligible to receive divine love, you simply must attach your mind to the objects of the divine realm. Everything we are trying to understand is to make us eligible candidates to receive love, and it will be given automatically by the Guru, without our asking or even wanting, when we are internally pure.

The Effort of Saints

In the world, agents are always canvassing prospective buyers for their products, even though people may be unwilling to pay their commission. Similarly, Saints always try to get more lovers for God, for His pleasure. They remain ever hopeful that a person will become eligible for their grace. They remain ever watchful and constantly endeavour to help souls move forward, and no matter how many times a soul may fall, they do not lose hope or give up in their endeavour. Worldly souls are always making mistakes and committing offences, but the Saints remain optimistic and keep forgiving them and pursuing them. Why? The answer is the same as in the case of God: it is their innate nature.

The Saint endeavours to take the soul on his spiritual journey as far as possible in this life, anticipating, 'He will continue in his next life and complete the journey.' He never gives up. He remains eternally hopeful for the soul. If you had the same job, you would give up in seconds. Imagine he works selflessly for people, and they constantly criticise him. 'How selfish he is! How greedy he is!' And the Saint, knowing all that goes on, remains silent. 'It is all right. Say whatever you want, my dear son, but I will not give up on you.' This is the nature of the Saints, causelessly merciful.

It is not that they have singled you out especially for their favour; they act according to their nature, and we act according to ours. Someone may be determined to commit *namaparadha*,[1] the gravest of all spiritual transgressions, even if the consequence is hell for millions of lifetimes. Do you know the consequences of thinking against God, the Saints or your Guru? 'Yes, I have heard, but I cannot avoid it. Though I repent later and shed tears, it continues to happen nevertheless.' But the Saints ignore your downfall after you commit such transgressions. When a child starts walking, he falls many times, but the parents do not lose hope. They know that he is only learning and that one day he will walk. It took you so long to learn the alphabet and days longer before you could write your own name. Have you forgotten the effort it took you to learn to write a single letter? So why give up hope in the divine area? Attach your mind to divine objects.

Worldly Love

This love is of three kinds:

1. Love for your own happiness
2. Love for the happiness of the Beloved and
3. Love for the happiness of both yourself and the Beloved

Love for Your Own Happiness

The first type of love towards God or the Saint is for your own happiness. You will claim that you already know this type of love. But no, you do not. If you had ever practised this level of love, you would not be in the condition you find yourself in now. This is the lowest level of love in the divine realm, but you have not been able to practise even this. I have strongly opposed this kind of love in my *Prema Rasa Madira*.[2] There must be more than seven or eight thousand lines in my literary works opposing this type of selfish devotion. I have given no importance to those Saints who practised this type of devotion. However, these are God-realised Saints that I am talking about, not ordinary souls under *maya*. People like Draupadi, Gajaraja, etc.

To love a Saint or God with a selfish motive is not wrong but should nevertheless be rejected, even though it will take you beyond *maya* and help you attain God and divine love. It is my recommendation that you do not practise this type of love, even by mistake.

Saints state that selfish devotion to Shri Krishna is superior to selfless love for celestials or human beings. This is because devotion to Shri Krishna will take you beyond *maya*, to His divine abode and grant you divine love, whereas devotion anywhere else will only reward you with whatever that person possesses.

यान्ति देवव्रता देवान्पितॄन्यान्ति पितृव्रताः।
भूतानि यान्ति भूतेज्या यान्ति मद्याजिनोऽपि माम्॥ (*Gita* 9.25)

Devotion to celestial gods will take you to celestial regions, which is temporary. Your goal of rising above material miseries and attaining eternal bliss will not be realised there. This desire to rid yourself of misery is a lower-realm goal. Even this cannot be realised because the object of your devotion is under *maya*.

Therefore, the very first condition for a lover is that he should not love for his own happiness. At present, you love for your own pleasure in the world, but this kind of love has no place in loving God. You are so well practised at this that it has almost become your nature, and yet, it is an obstacle in going towards God.

The Art of Deceit

Every second, a wife plans how to meet her selfish needs through her husband. 'How should I stand? How should I look at him? How should I speak to him so that I get what

I want from him?' The husband, too, is thinking of ways to fool his wife so that she remains in his control and keeps providing him with all the facilities and pleasures of his choice. In other words, both want to be the other's object of devotion.

Now when both parties are trying to occupy one seat, there is bound to be conflict at every moment. What is it that we have done all our lives? We have learned the various arts and sciences of deceiving people, and the person most adept at doing this is considered the most advanced or the smartest. 'He is such an expert that he can turn anyone in his favour (and then exploit him for his own ends).' What we call etiquette in the world is the art of cleverly and shrewdly speaking and behaving to get our work done and our needs met in the world.

A person manages to get something out of another, which he has not given to someone else, all because of how he was approached: his gestures, his expressions and his behaviour. What people call civilised is gross cheating, sham or show. It is in our preoccupation with this that we waste the energy of our entire life. We pick up this shrewdness, this cunningness by reading novels, books and newspapers, and by associating with people who are experts in dealing with the world. With this accumulated knowledge, we become experts at duping our husbands, wives, parents, children and neighbours, and then the rest of the world. But what does all this do for us? We gain more of the material world for ourselves, but we do not attain happiness from this. And what is the result of your lifetime of effort? You have never thought about it.

God's Anger

God and the Saints are two personalities who can do nothing but shower mercy. As people, you can do whatever you want, show anger, etc. But this is not the case with God. What about Shishupal, whose head was cut off by Shri Krishna or Ravana, who was killed by Shri Rama and Bhishma, whom Shri Krishna attacked with a chariot wheel? This was not anger; this was an act. Anger is something felt within, not something shown externally. These were all cases of acting, and it is done not only by God but also by His Saints. Arjuna and Hanumana, for example, killed millions of people. Such acting is child's play for them. What did Ravana say at the time of his death, caused by Shri Rama's so-called anger? 'For as long as I lived, You could not set foot in Lanka and now I am going to Your abode before You. Whose victory was it — Yours or mine?' Shri Rama remained silent because His anger was a mere act. If His anger had been genuine, then there would have been no need for a prolonged drama. He could have flicked the switch from within, and Ravana would have died instantly, and He could have sent him to hell.

But He collected this huge force of monkeys and bears and did all kinds of things instead. In truth, however, the special power of determining the death of anyone is in His hands. He just has to withdraw the life force and the person will die. He just has to order Yamaraja, 'Let him spend millions of ages in hell for his misbehaviour,' and it will happen. But none of that happened, and Ravana instead attained His divine abode. Can this really be called anger? No. It is mercy.

Thus, what have we done wrong? We are at least better than Ravana, yet we are moving through the endless cycle of birth and death across the 8.4 million species of life while Ravana attains His abode! Because towards us, there is neither mercy nor anger; He remains neutral.

समोऽहं सर्वभूतेषु न मे द्वेष्योऽस्ति न प्रिय:। (*Gita* 9.29)

I am equal to everyone, and I sit in everyone's heart and note his ideas of every moment. This is all I do. I do not disturb anyone. You can do or think whatever pleases you. I just maintain your record and grant you the fruits of your actions.

Why doesn't He kill us like Ravana and give us His abode? No, that is reserved for those who are deserving. Ravana knew who He was.

खरदूषण मो सम बलवंता। तिन्हहिं को मारइ बिनु भगवंता॥
(*Rama Charita Manasa*)

Ravana says, 'Khara and Dushana had strength equivalent to mine, and no one can kill them except God. And they have been killed by Rama. This means He is a descension of God.'

Ravana, therefore, decided to oppose Rama, to fight Him and attain his goal. Everyone played their part in this way, and the people were unaware of what was really happening. It is like when you watch a film or play: nothing happens by chance. Everything is well rehearsed many days before.

The same is true for the pastimes of God; everything is planned well in advance.

Consequence of Greed

King Srinjaya and Sage Narada

There is a story in the *Mahabharata* of a king called Srinjaya. He went to Sage Narada and begged him to bestow his grace. Saints like Sage Narada just bestow grace on others, because there is nothing else they do or can do. Srinjaya asked Sage Narada for the boon of a son. Sage Narada thought to himself, 'Look at this foolish request! He wants a son. Over the course of infinite lives, sometimes he has one son, sometimes two, sometimes ten and sometimes fifty – the time when he had the body of a lower species (animals). He has had so many sons in infinite lives and he is still not satisfied! Anyway, so be it. He has not asked for anything big.' 'Go, you will have a son.' 'No, no. Wait, there is a condition. I want a son whose body only expels gold from every part.' In other words, everything he excretes, spits out or which comes out normally as part of a bodily function should be gold. Sage Narada smiled to himself. 'He is inviting calamity upon himself.' However, Sage Narada granted him a son who was called Suvarnashtheevi, the one whose body excretes gold.

Twice daily he would excrete half a kilo of gold, and anything else that came out of his body – mucus or any other excretion – would also turn to gold. Even his perspiration would be gold! The king started using his gold liberally; even his palace was made of gold. Such reckless extravagance soon attracted the attention of thieves. Even if one is a king, there is still a limit to his wealth. It could increase somewhat, and in his case, it was increasing daily, something that could not remain hidden for long. When someone confides in someone else, he in turn confides in someone else, and in time, the word spreads out.

Soon, everyone knew about the king's secret, including the thieves who came and abducted his son. To defeat the king's army, many thieves had to conspire together. When the question regarding the division of the spoils came up, it was suggested that, as they were twelve in number, every twelfth day, one thief should get the gold the son excretes from his body. But there was disagreement and they began squabbling among themselves. Finally, they decided to divide the king's son into twelve pieces. They went ahead and did that and, of course, no one got any gold. The prince was dead, the king was now without a son and the thieves were left empty-handed.

The dreadful consequences of desiring material objects are evident to everyone.

Until now, you have practised only one thing – loving the *mayic* world and that too only for our own benefit.

न वा अरे सर्वस्य कामाय सर्वं प्रियं भवत्यात्मनस्तु कामाय सर्वं प्रियं भवति।
(Brihadaranyaka Upanishad)

The *Vedas* issue a challenge that it is impossible for any individual to love without self-interest until God-realisation. Prior to that, every thought and everything you do practically will be rooted only in self-interest. When you proclaim, 'I want to help you,' what is it really? You want to give help worth one rupee now so that you can make a 100-rupee profit from that person later. This kind of help is just a sham, yet nowadays, this is what we call doing someone a favour or obliging someone. When there is a flood or some other calamity, public money is allocated to relieve the distressed public. But what happens? Those involved divvy up the money among themselves. 'You take this much per cent and you take this much.' Of course, some money is given to the public, and signatures are collected as proof of how much has been given. Thus, our love in this world is purely based only on our self-interest. What we have done in the world, are doing and will do has only one goal behind it – self-interest.

Despite doing everything at every moment only for our own self-interest, no one is ready to admit that they are selfish. Someone says, 'You are selfish,' and we snap back angrily, 'What did you say?' In other words, we are not ready to hear this word. Daily, I tell you to practise humility, to abandon pride and shed tears, but you do not do it. You do not accept this teaching.

Faults and Criticism

There was a Saint called Pundarikaksha, with a disciple called Rama Mishra. Once, the disciple asked his Guru, 'Why have I not attained God? Why does my mind not go to Him?' The Guru asked him, 'Why do you ask these questions?' 'Because I want to attain God.' 'You are lying! If you had a genuine desire to attain God, you would have attained your goal. You are just asking for the sake of asking. Anyway, will you do whatever I say? You have not fostered humility within yourself, nor do you have the right emotions, nor do you shed any tears. Do you know the remedy for this? You should hide the faults of others and advertise your own faults to them.'

Rama Mishra thought to himself, 'I have done everything except this. I do hide my faults, fearing what people will say, or I restrict it to God and Guru – I confess my sins to them.' But even from the Guru, you expect that he will not repeat it to others or else your relationship with him will end. The Guru said, 'There is no need to tell me. Proclaim your faults before others and never think of anyone else's faults or speak about them.'

Pay close attention. This is the reason you are stuck. You want the praise of others. You fight amongst each other over mere words. 'He called me this!' Who are you anyway? What status can you lay claim to? Whatever anyone says applies to you. In fact, the person could have said a lot more. What has been said so far is insignificant.

You are a storehouse of infinite offences and you are committing new ones every second, and yet if someone singles out one or two, it becomes intolerable for you. You are not ready to hear the truth. The fact is that this person is benefitting you by bringing your attention to your faults, and yet you see it as an offence.

When two *satsangis* get together, they criticise other *satsangis*: 'Oh, this person did this and that *satsangi* said that.' Why don't you vow to speak to other *satsangis* only about God and Guru? If someone tries to speak with you on some other subject, then tell them politely but firmly, 'This is against the Guru's wish. If you bring it up again,

I will not come here anymore.' If someone speaks against someone in your family, be it your wife or sister, you do not visit that house again. Then how can you tolerate something said against another *satsangi*? Then, in turn, you repeat it to someone else. After all this, you come to me saying, 'Maharaj Ji, I have not made any progress.' If you do not want to move forward, what can anyone do? Try and follow this teaching of Pundarikaksha and display your own faults and hide those of others. True humility will come from doing so, and this is the very foundation of devotion. Then you will definitely move forward.

Understanding Selfish Love

Thus, selfish love is of two kinds: (1) loving God and Guru for some worldly gain and (2) loving the world for some worldly gain.

We are familiar with the second type of love. In fact, it is all that we have ever done over infinite lives. The knowledge that you currently have is not just from one single life. I told you earlier that the five working senses, the five knowledge-acquiring senses and the five life airs, along with the mind, intellect and ego, all these eighteen elements accompany the soul even after death. This intellect of yours is the product of infinite lives of nurturing. But all that your intellect has learned so far is what it should do regarding worldly people to meet worldly ends. You use your intellect to do this; sometimes you succeed, sometimes you get partial results, and sometimes none at all. At times, the opposite happens

– you fail. However, you continue to make efforts in this direction and remain committed.

Therefore, it is not surprising that your love for the world arises solely from selfish desires. What is surprising, however, is that you continue to rely on the material world to fulfil them. Imagine if you directed the same intensity of selfish love towards Shri Krishna as Draupadi did in her moment of helplessness or as Gajaraja did with his heart full of fear and with complete surrender. Their devotion, though born of self-interest, was turned towards the Supreme Power. In contrast, our desires are tied solely to the world, and thus, they are never truly fulfilled.

You Become What You Love

Our mind can be equated to a girl who inherits the property of the boy she marries.

Those individuals who loved God selfishly did not know Him as God and did not accept Him in that way. Many *gopis* loved Shri Krishna the way a worldly woman loves a man. People like Kamsa got attached to Him through fear and some souls considered Him a relative.

गोप्य: कामाद्द्रयात्कंसो द्वेषाच्चैद्यादयो नृपा:। (*Bhagavatam* 7.1.30)

The *gopis* attained Krishna through love, Kamsa through fear, and kings like Shishupala through hatred.

Whether someone gently touches iron to a touchstone or angrily strikes it with an iron hammer, in both cases the iron will turn into gold. In the same way, whether you love God selfishly or selflessly, the result will be divine. Let's take an example: suppose you love your father but are unaware that he has been a great sinner. If, as a result of his sinful actions, he is born into a lower species, then you, too, would be bound to become his child in that same species.

'Why should that happen? I have just been devoted to my father?' But wherever your father goes, you will have to go. This is the spiritual law.

यान्ति देवव्रता देवान्पितॄन्यान्ति पितृव्रता: ।
भूतानि यान्ति भूतेज्या यान्ति मद्याजिनोऽपि माम् ॥ (*Gita* 9.25)

The *Gita* proclaims, 'After death, you will attain the same personality of the one you love in this birth.'

A great liberated and pure soul like Jada Bharata had to become a deer in his next life because of the attachment he had to a fawn. He felt compassion for the fawn after witnessing the death of its mother and adopted it, and slowly he became attached to it.

Nowadays, grandmothers take their grandchildren into their laps and roam around with them. What are you doing these days? 'Oh, nothing much.' All your responsibilities are over, and your sons and daughters are all married. So how much devotion do you practise? 'Oh, I do not do any *bhajan*. I have three or four little grandchildren.' And they are so attached to them. Speaking to them in baby talk, they fondly remark, 'He is such a little rascal!' And, of course, his mother hears this and feels overwhelmed with joy. 'Oh, they care so much for my child.' Is it possible for someone to love anyone else's child other than their own? People act in this way all the time and mothers get fooled repeatedly, thinking that so-and-so loves their child so much. Of course, you must do whatever is necessary, but these grandmothers get so attached that they start worrying about them. Of course, this is not surprising.

If a *paramahamsa* like Jada Bharata could get so attached to a fawn that he had to become a deer in his next life, then there are clearly no exceptions to this rule. In fact, you will attain that to which you were attached in this birth in your next life. Those who love God and the Saint will therefore attain a divine result. This is an absolute certainty.

केमा: स्त्रियो वनचरीर्व्यभिचारदुष्टा: कृष्णे क्व चैष परमात्मनि रूढभाव:।
नन्वीश्वरोऽनुभजतोऽविदुषोऽपि साक्षाच्छ्रेयस्तनोत्यगदराज इवोपयुक्त:॥

(Bhagavatam 10.47.59)

Shukadeva Paramahamsa explains this principle very clearly to Parikshit. Parikshit asked his Guru, 'Many of the *gopis* who loved Shri Krishna did not even consider Him to be a Saint, let alone God. Their attraction was like that of a woman for a man, seeing His mischievous nature, His beauty or His flute playing, and so on. This is the state of a soul in ignorance. How then did they reach such an exalted position?'

Shukadeva understood what he meant and said, 'Your mind is so morally corrupt that it can only have ideas related to the material world.'

We often take medicine for different problems. Tell me, how are these medicines made? 'I don't have the slightest idea. I have never seen one being made.' 'But does it benefit you?' 'Yes.' 'And the person who makes the medicine also takes it when he has the same problem, and it benefits him equally. He does not benefit more because he knows the constitution of the medicine.'

An illiterate rustic is told to take one white pill followed by one black pill. He does not even know the name of what he is taking and yet the medicine will benefit him in the same way it would to others who know about it. We can understand, therefore, that the substance of something does its work irrespective of our knowledge or ignorance of it.

Similarly, if your mind gets attached to Shri Krishna as your father, your son or even as your enemy, you will derive a divine benefit. You will acquire His property – liberation from *maya*, divine love, His divine abode and whatever else He has. This will all happen just like the benefits of taking medicine, irrespective of your knowledge, or the lack thereof, of its constitution.

The person who knows Shri Krishna to be the Almighty God cannot love Him. He will instead have to accept the five devotional relationships – *bhavas*. He is my master, and I am His servant. Higher than this, He is my friend, followed by He is my child and finally, He is my Beloved. If you think of Him as Almighty God you will not be able to relish the parental sentiments that His mother, Yashoda, experienced or the special sweetness of the *madhurya bhava* the *gopis* had for Shri Krishna. Instead, there will be fear, distance and reservations in your relationship, even if you have a selfish motive with a loving sentiment.

Love of any kind directed towards anyone in this world under the bondage of *maya*, whether as your father, your daughter, your son, your husband or any other relationship, will only bind you to the realm of *maya*. 'I love this person as a daughter. Is that a sin?' Yes, it is. You have no right to love anyone else in the world. You have a daughter. That is all right. Nurture her, feed her, clothe her and educate her. Do your duty. This is your responsibility, but you are not here to love her.

मामेकं शरणं व्रज। (Gita 18.66)
Shri Krishna declares, 'Surrender to Me alone.'

त्वमेव सर्वं मम देव देव। (Veda Vyasa)
Veda Vyasa states, 'O Lord! You alone are everything to me.'

You have only one mind and if that is attached to the world, with which mind will you love the Saint and God? If you say, 'I will love both,' then this is like rinsing your clothes alternately in clean water and then in dirty water. What is the benefit? Love God a little and love the world a little. Shedding two tears when you leave your Guru and shedding two more when your daughter leaves you is mere jocularity.

The Love of Surdasa

You must have heard of a Saint called Surdasa, who was blind from birth. One day, he came across a well that had no boundary around it, causing him to fall into it. He used to move about on his own, begging for food while chanting 'Radhe Radhe'. Shri Krishna personally came to pull him out of the well. Surdasa experienced something different in Shri Krishna's touch, different from all the worldly touches he had experienced, and so he firmly grabbed hold of His hand, suspecting it was his Beloved's. When Shri Krishna freed Himself with a jerk, Surdasa said, 'What greatness have You shown in freeing Yourself from the grip of an old man, who sustains himself by begging and is weakened from falling down a well? If You genuinely want to show that You are all-powerful, then show it by leaving my heart.'

हस्तमाक्षिप्य यातोऽसि बलात् कृष्ण किमद्भुतम्।
हृदयाद्यदि निर्यासि पौरुषं गणयामि ते॥

(Vilvamangala, *Krishnakarnamrita* 3.96)

The very next day, both Shri Radha and Shri Krishna came hoping to hear him say something. Shri Krishna warned Radha Rani, 'Stay some distance from him, otherwise he will grab hold of Your foot. Blind people do not let go of things easily.' Radha Rani said, 'It is all right if he catches Me. I will go with him.' Shri Krishna replied, 'As You wish, but I will not come to free You.' Radha Rani slowly moved towards Surdasa and the sound of Her anklets tinkling reached his ears. Blind people develop a subtle sense of hearing because their mind is so focused on it to compensate for the lack of sight.

Surdasa knew someone was moving carefully towards him, but he acted as though he did not know anything. When She was very close, and the tinkling of Her anklets had stopped, he lunged forward to catch hold of what was in front of him. But Radha Rani was vigilant, having been warned by Shri Krishna that this might happen. As a result, She was able to step back and avoid getting caught. However, he was able to grab one of Her anklets.

Surdasa thought, 'Oh well, I will make the best of a bad bargain.' Shri Krishna said, 'I had warned You. I once had a similar experience with him.' Now Radha Rani had to go for *raas*[3] at that time, so She said, 'Surdasa, please return My anklet. I have to go for *raas*.' Surdasa said, 'Look, I am blind. I cannot be sure that what I have is Yours. There may be several other women standing here and if I give it to one, then another may blame me for it. You first give me my eyesight so that I may recognise You, in case someone asks me to identify who I gave it to.' Shri Krishna said to Radha Rani mockingly, 'Look, I had warned You earlier.'

Finally, Surdasa was granted vision. What effort was it for Them to do so? Surdasa got to see Shri Radha–Krishna. As is the custom upon attaining God and seeing Them for the first time, They said, 'Ask for a boon.' Shri Krishna looked at Radha Rani, 'Let us see what he asks for.' Surdasa replied, 'These eyes have seen You for the first time, and I have seen nothing else with them. I have no desire to see the world with these eyes after this, so please take away my eyesight and make me blind again.' Tears rolled down the eyes of Shri Krishna. After all, He is bound by the love of His devotees, and so He had to fulfil Surdasa's wish of making him blind again.

6

He Alone Is Mine

YOU WERE TOLD ABOUT the beloved, *premaspada*, the lover, *premi*, and love, *prema*. Beloved is someone who possesses divine love, God's most confidential personal power, which can be attained only through the grace of a Rasika Saint. Divine love is not something that can be attained through personal effort; even great yogis, *munis* and *paramahamsas* desire this. However, the treasure house of this divine love is Shri Krishna and His associates, the Saints, and no one else.

No one under *maya* can occupy the seat of *premaspada*, not even if he holds the seat of the king of celestials. If someone is controlled by *maya*, then it is absolutely apparent that divine love has not been attained by him. One who is devoid of divine love cannot assume the seat of *premaspada*, that is, be the object of love — the beloved. Therefore, no worldly soul can be *premaspada*. Without cultivating the relationship between the servant and the master, you cannot attain your goal.

तस्यैवाहं ममैवासौ स एवाहमिति त्रिधा।
भगवच्छरणार्थित्वं साधनाभ्यासपाकत:॥ (Madhusudan Sarasvati)

In the above verse, three types of surrender or love have been described: (1) I am His; (2) He is mine; and (3) I am Him.

The first two kinds of love can be practised. The third kind of love is a special state where the relationship of servant with the master ends.

I Am Him

In these three philosophies, I am Him is not a philosophy but a description of a certain elevated state. While meditating on the Beloved, one becomes so immersed that he starts feeling he is the Beloved himself. This is a very advanced state.

Ramakrishna Paramahamsa

He would lift a garland to put on Mother Kali and say, 'O Mother! O Mother! O Mother!' and he would put it around his own neck. He would consider himself to be the Divine Mother. This is not acting, or done consciously, but done in a state of non-duality. There is an evolved state of love where the servant thinks himself to be the master and the master thinks himself to be the servant.

Lord Rama and Hanumana

You must have heard or read in the *Ramayana* where Lord Rama is sitting under a tree and Hanumana and various other divine personalities are seated on the branches above. Pay attention. Lord Rama's descension was to establish *maryada* – the decorum and propriety of conduct – where Bharata[1] is describing the qualities of a servitor as:

सिर बल चलौं धरम अस मोरा। सब ते सेवक धर्म कठोरा॥ (*Ramayana*)

A servant should place his head wherever his master's feet
tread.

Hanumana and many others are embodiments of the sentiment
of servitorship or *dasya bhava*. They are not *madhurya bhava*
Saints who can act as they please and take liberties with God.
But here they are acting in this way and neither does Lord
Rama feel bad about it nor does He chastise them by saying,
'What kind of misbehaviour is this, sitting above Me? If you
do not want to sit below Me, then at least sit on the same
level.' They are in the jungle, and so there is no throne at a
higher level. In such circumstances, you cannot sit lower, so
you therefore have a valid reason to sit on the same level as
your master. But here they are sitting above His head, on the
very tree under which Lord Rama is sitting.

Now did this happen accidentally? No, they are absorbed in a
devotional trance where Hanumana and associates are thinking,
'We are the master,' and Lord Rama, in turn, is thinking, 'I
am their servant.' This is the very same Lord Rama who took
propriety to the extreme limit by cutting off Shurpanakha's nose
for breach of etiquette. How did such behaviour take place?
Not a single person was in a normal state of consciousness. If
they were, then one could have pointed out to the others what
was going on. Even a sensible person in a group can talk some
sense into the rest. But they were all in a special state of *samadhi*.

I Am His

He is mine and I am His. These are two different principles
which describe two sentiments — You have eternally been

mine and I am eternally Yours. But there is one point here. The sentiment that He is mine is superior. He is mine, that is all. I do not care whether I am His or not. Besides, there is no doubt that I am His because I am a part of Him. According to the *Vedas*, I have an eternal natural relationship with Him and cannot be anyone else's.

The scriptures unanimously declare that no one else can have any relationship with the soul: 'The soul is an eternal part of God. All relationships are with Him alone.'

चनिमात्रं श्री हरेरंशम्
धाता माता पितामह: (*Gita* 9.17)

I am the father of this universe, the mother, the sustainer and the grandfather as well.

There is no conflict over this — I am His. But nothing has been achieved by us from this so far. Infinite lives have gone by — I was His, I am His and I will always be His. This has been proclaimed by Shri Krishna personally and has been declared in the *Vedas* too, but to no avail. Now how will we get results? The answer is in the sentiment 'He is mine', which arises only when we accept Him as our own wholeheartedly.

He Is Mine

Those fortunate souls, Tulsidasa, Surdasa, Mira, Kabira, Nanaka and Tukarama, who accepted Him as theirs, attained the goal, transcended *maya* and attained the ultimate bliss of divine love. And those who have not yet realised this fact are moving through the endless cycle of life and death across the 8.4 million species of life. We should develop the feeling that 'He alone is mine'. In other words, no one else but He is mine. It is certainly incorrect to say that He is mine alone.

The day the sentiment that 'He alone is mine' becomes firmly established in you, instead of 'He is mine alone', you will achieve your goal. After this, there is nothing more to be done – no *karma*, no *jnana*, no *bhakti* – nothing! The final action for the individual soul is to accept that He alone is mine, after which everything will be attained, and you will be freed from *maya* forever. By accepting it, all problems will come to an end.

Reciprocation of Love

Whoever you love – father, son, husband or wife – you are constantly wondering whether they love you back. Why are you worried about this? Regardless of whether the person loves you or not, why don't you continue to love him or her? 'I am not that foolish to love someone when there is no reciprocation. To hell with such love! I wrote four letters and did not get a single reply. I vow never to write to him again.'

'I sent four letters, and he sent me eight in reply! He really does love me!' Just look at your method of measuring love – based on external behaviour. This is such foolishness and the reason why worldly people take advantage of you. If you want perfect reciprocation for your love, then you will not be able to love at all, because if the love of the other party reduces, so will yours. If the other becomes neutral, so will you. If they oppose you, then you will have to oppose them. What happened to your love? Everything has become topsy-turvy. This is not love.

A child loves rasagulla. Does the child ever think, 'Does the rasagulla love me too? I have shed tears in front of my mother and father to get it.' No. Whether the rasagulla loves me or not, what business is it of mine? I like the taste of it and so I love it. In the same way, if we love someone, why do we want to know whether that person loves us in return? If we do, then this is not love but sheer deception. It is just a business transaction. 'I gave him ten rupees, but he did not give me ten rupees worth of goods in return.' Instantly, you are perturbed. 'He only gave me vegetables worth five rupees! At the very least, I should receive ten rupees worth of goods.' Now if he gives you ₹11 worth of vegetables, then you feel a special kind of joy.

It is this worldly business sense that we apply in our dealings of love. We make such a big effort to show how much we love a person, but all the while, we have the internal sentiment of wanting to receive more love from them in return. On the other hand, if you focus only on the idea 'He alone is mine', you will not be in this constant dilemma.

The Irrefutable Law

You may well ask, 'Am I His or not? Does He consider me His or not? Does He love me or not?' Just remember one principle always. This is the verdict of the scriptures, the *Vedas* and the *Puranas*, and it is also said by God Himself.

ये यथा मां प्रपद्यन्ते तांस्तथैव भजाम्यहम्। (*Gita* 4.11)

This is an irrefutable divine principle: 'I reciprocate the love of a soul to the exact degree and with the exact sentiment that he loves Me.'

This is an indisputable, unchanging law. When this is God's irrefutable law, why worry about whether He outwardly shows love or not? He will have to love. God is not some worldly person who, after listening to some third party speaking against us, stops loving us or reduces His love. Why is there any doubt? He is all-seeing and all-knowing. He is the witness of everything, the well-wisher of all, the Lord of all and the all-powerful. There is no shadow of doubt regarding this, especially since it is His law that no power can shake or disturb the degree and amount of His love. God is unwavering when it comes to His laws, so this is definite.

There is no need to think about whether He loves you or not, or how much He loves you. He loves you as much as you love Him. So how much love do you want? 'Lots.' Okay, then love Him a lot. But if you love Him a little and want a lot, how will this be possible? And if your love is just business, even then you will have to remember that you cannot get a 1,000-rupee sari for ₹10. Just look at the value of what you have to offer and expect a return according to your investment. The sari is available for anyone who is willing to pay ₹1,000 to buy it. The shopkeeper does not care whether the buyer is a Saint, a sweeper, a Brahmin or a prime minister.

God loves you to the extent you love and surrender to Him. When you truly understand this law, you will not worry about whether He considers you His or not. 'Does He love me, and if so, how much?' All such questions will cease. All the speculation prevalent in the world today is because people are not all-knowing, and thus they are easily confused if someone speaks something against them. Everyone has imperfections. And in the world, love is measured by external behaviour. But the one who is seated within, noting all your ideas, cannot make such mistakes. So the question of doubt in His case cannot arise.

God's Love

We therefore must keep to the sentiment 'He alone is mine'. And, of course, that we are His. If you want to say both, then that is all right too. But be careful in your use of the word 'alone'. He *alone* is mine is correct, but He is mine *alone* is incorrect. He has infinite souls, and you are just one of them. If a million souls love Him simultaneously up to a certain limit, then He would love all of them to that exact same limit. He possesses this ability. Even a worldly mother and father have the capacity to reciprocate the love of four or five children and no one complains when they do. 'Who do you love the most out of us four brothers?' 'I love all four of you.' 'How is that possible?' You have five fingers on your hand and each one experiences pain when your hand is squeezed too hard. All five fingers are washed with soap and cleaned. Thus, all five fingers are loved. No one loves just one finger. When an ordinary worldly mother can show love towards four, six or ten children, then what is not possible for the all-powerful God, the governor of *yogamaya*, who can take on unlimited forms? There is no problem for Him at all.

You should not worry yourself with all this, and you should not desire that He should love you alone. The Saints are constantly thinking that God should love others, whether He loves them or not. In other words, they love Him without even wanting Him to love them in return.

Had he not made this law of loving us as much as we love Him, what do you think you have that is so special that He would love you for it? You have a filthy body with nine orifices through which nothing but filth comes out. As a matter of fact, foul-smelling perspiration flows from each pore of your body. Our *mayic* bodies are made of the five material elements, whereas He has a transcendental blissful form. What reason could He possibly have to even look in your direction? Your body is a filthy bag of five gross elements, and yet you recoil when you look at a pile of garbage. You marvel at the sight of a manicured flower garden with beautiful fragrant roses and lotuses in full bloom and are repulsed by the sight of a heap of refuse placed next to it. What is this refuse? Just something else made of the five material elements, of which your eyes are also made and so too are those flowers. It is this same garbage that will fertilise those flowers and help them bloom.

All of this is material and constitutes different combinations of the same elements to look different. They are all the same. But you do not want to look at all of them. And yet the divine, all-knowing Lord should look at our material bodies and our dirty material minds and love us? You, mere material beings, are not even ready to love someone ordinary, let alone someone below your status.

Obsessed with the External

Once, a prince became besotted by a girl called Yogashila, who was the daughter of a Brahmin. The king requested the Brahmin to have his daughter married to his son. Under any normal circumstance, a father would consider it great fortune that his daughter could marry a prince, because she would be marrying into royalty. But the father objected because he was a Brahmin and the prince was a Kshatriya.

The king insisted, 'If you want to continue living in my kingdom, then you have to give your daughter's hand in marriage to my son.' Seeing her father troubled, Yogashila consoled him, 'Don't worry. Tell them that I will be ready to marry the prince in two weeks.' 'This will happen over my dead body,' retorted her father. But Yogashila was insistent, 'Be patient, Father, and see what I can do in two weeks.'

Using her yogic powers, she reduced her body weight until she was mere skin and bones. She then smeared filth all over her body. When the prince returned, he said, 'Is this some sick joke? Where is the girl I fell in love with?' Yogashila said, 'I am that girl.' 'How can that be? She had beautiful limbs and flesh covering her body; she had beauty and lustre.' Yogashila replied, 'If you love flesh, go to a butcher's shop where a lot of flesh is sold. If you love me, then here I am.'

Now forget about a prince, not even a pauper would be ready to marry a girl with no flesh on her body! And so Yogashila was saved. Here, I am merely pointing out that in this world, when someone loves a person based on external aspects – such as outer appearance and form – then the moment those external qualities fade, the love also comes to an end. A boy and a girl are madly in love but after marriage and having children, as time passes, and when the body has lost its physical appeal, they start fighting! Then they say to each other, 'I was deceived by you and now my life is ruined as a result of marrying you,' and so on and so forth. This is happening in almost every household. I think all of you must have heard about this and must have had practical experience with it as well.

The Madness of Mistaken Identity

So what do we have to do to attract the attention of God? Our body is filthy, our mind is impure, and as for the intellect, the less said the better! Even after infinite lives, we still do not know whether we are the body or the soul. We may be highly educated, holding prestigious degrees, postgraduate or doctorate, but we still do not know who we are.

Ask anyone in the world, 'Who are you?' 'I am a collector.' I am not asking about your post; I am asking about who you are. 'Ramesh Shukla.' Not your name; who are you? 'I am a man.' This is the designation of your body; who are you? 'I don't know anything beyond this.' You do not know who you are! A person in the world who does not know who he is is certified insane by a doctor. Considered potentially dangerous, he is sent and locked up in a mental asylum and the government spends money to keep him there so that no harm is caused to the public.

All of us are living in a mental asylum. In fact, this whole world is a mental asylum. There are 8.4 million types of cells (bodies) made by God's government and individual souls are put into the bodies they deserve. The body of a dog, cat, ass, human and celestial god are all included in this mental asylum. You may claim, 'But I do not consider myself mad.' But when has a madman ever realised that he is mad? If you ask him, he will say, 'You are mad. I am perfectly fine.'

The moment a person becomes aware of his situation, his work is done. The moment one realises he is ignorant, the desire for knowledge comes and he acquires knowledge of the self. And right now, what happens? We say, 'We do not have the time.' People often prioritise worldly matters over listening to spiritual teachings.

All these millionaires come to me and ask, 'Maharaj Ji, please grace me.' What type of grace? 'Divine.' Then, for that, you will need to give me some of your time. 'But Maharaj Ji, we just don't have any time. I have so many mills and factories in so many states. I cannot spare even a second.' Then this just proves that you do not have the yearning, so find your happiness in the world. Such a person still has faith that happiness lies there. Why come to me? When you fully realise that even the king of celestials cannot attain an iota of peace or happiness in his dreams, only then should you come to me.

You think that Saints have some kind of a magic wand and that they can do whatever they like? If God or the Saints could do that, then why would this material world exist? They could just wave their magic wand and grant infinite spiritual happiness to all the souls in all the infinite universes!

God and the Saints are *satya-sankalpa* after all — whatever they desire, happens. But has any Saint done this until today? If they had done so, why would the world continue to exist? Since this world does remain, how can you harbour hopes like these? There is something that you also must do.

True Yearning

You must make the sentiment 'He alone is mine' firm, whether it takes you one month, one year, one lifetime or ten lifetimes. You must increase your attachment to God and consider that 'He alone is mine' to the extent that:

युगायितं निमेषेण चक्षुषा प्रावृषायितम्। शून्यायितं जगत् सर्वं गोविन्दविरहेण मे॥

(Gauranga Mahaprabhu, Shikchashtak 7)

'My beloved Krishna! A moment of separation seems like millions of years have passed without seeing You. Tears from my eyes never stop for a moment. The whole world seems desolate and void. There remains no charm for me. O my beloved Govinda! Your separation has made me so.' Only when you reach the deepest state of separation does the true yearning for God's attainment begin.

Symptoms of Deep Love

आहे सर्दो रंगे ज़र्दो चश्मेतर इन्तज़ारी बेकरारी ब्रेसबर।
कम गुफ़्तनों कम ख़ुर्दनो ख़्वाबेहराम आशिकारा नौनिशां।

A beautiful Persian poem depicts nine symptoms that describe someone suffering from deep love or longing:

1. Taking deep, cold sighs
2. A pale complexion – the complexion turns yellowish in the fire of separation
3. Tearful eyes – tears constantly flow from the eyes
4. Waiting for the Beloved
5. Restlessness

6. Impatience
7. Speaking very little
8. Eating very little
9. Sleepless nights

Speaking Very Little

I emphasise this point every year and get upset because you people cannot control your talking.[2] You talk when I leave the meditation hall, thinking I do not know. This is your delusion. Yesterday, I abstained from eating in protest, and I do some similar atonement for your mistakes every year, but nothing seems to have any effect on you. None of you is content until you speak, knowing full well that I could act against you by asking you to leave. You are ready to leave, but you are not ready to stop speaking. Just think of the tremendous loss you are incurring. If you had love for God, you would not like anyone speaking to you; the words would seem like an arrow being shot into the ear. You would say, 'Keep quiet! While here, you should just chant God's name! Nothing else should be spoken or heard.' But no. You want to talk and listen to gossip about others.

Eating Very Little

Another point is that there should not be any attraction to food. And what do you people do? Some of you go out to buy delicacies because you are not satisfied with the simple pulses and vegetables served here. You could suffer from food poisoning from doing this, but you do not care about the possible consequences. Haven't you eaten sweets before? 'Oh, many times, but my mind wants it again.' Did you come here simply to satisfy your taste buds by obeying the dictates of your mind? One should eat the available food in moderation.

Sleepless Nights

Another symptom of love is the loss of sleep. If I say that everyone can go to sleep at 9 p.m. today, everyone will joyously repeat, 'All glories to Maharaj Ji! He is so merciful.' Only a few will think, 'That is a loss of two hours today. We could have had two more hours of *sadhana*. Oh well, since it is the Guru who has ordered it, I will sit up on my bed and engage my mind in loving remembrance up to the usual scheduled finishing time of 11.30 p.m.'[3] There are just a handful of people like this. But when this state comes, you will wholeheartedly say, 'There is so much bliss in this feeling of separation.' There is bliss in the tears of love, in the sighs and the pain of separation.

Someone who sees you crying might question, 'Are you experiencing some kind of trouble?' No, no. I am crying for my Beloved Lord. But he will say, 'It does not matter for whom you are crying; you have all the symptoms of grief!' 'You fool, these tears for the Lord are so precious that even the great *paramahamsas* yearn for them.'

But such things cannot be understood right now. When you reach these states and attain that bliss, then you will say, 'Out of union and separation, separation is superior because in separation you see your Beloved everywhere.'

सङ्गम विरह विकल्पे वरमिह विरहो न सङ्गमस्तस्मात्।
सङ्गे स इह तथैकस्त्रिभुवनमपि तन्मयं विरहे॥

(Gauranga Mahaprabhu)

Between the options of union and separation, I choose separation, not union. For in union, He is here, but in separation, the entire world is filled with His presence.

The Gopis of Braja

In the state of separation from Shri Krishna, the *gopis* of Braja saw Him everywhere, in all the living and non-living objects; in fact, all over Braja.

बाटन में घाटन में वीथिन में बागन में,
वृक्षन में बेलिन में वाटिका में वन में।
दरन में दिवारन में देहरी दरीचन में,
हीरन में हारन में भूषण में तन में॥
गोकुल में गायन में गोपिन में गोधन में,
याहि ब्रज मण्डल के रेनू में कन में।
जहाँ जहाँ देखौं तहाँ श्याम ही दिखाई देत,
मेरो श्याम छाय रह्यो नैनन में मन में॥ (Shaligram)

The poet Shaligram has described this very beautifully in the above verses: Wherever the *gopis* cast their eyes, they could only see their Beloved, Shri Krishna. In the lanes, on the riverbank, in the gardens, in the trees of Braja, in the vines that entwined the trees, in the flower beds, the forests, on the walls, on the steps, in precious stones, in necklaces, all over the village of Gokula, in the cows, in all ornaments and adornments, in themselves, and in every dust particle of Braja. In short, wherever the *gopis* looked, they could only see Shri Krishna. In this way, their Beloved Shri Krishna remained with them and in their minds always.

जित देखूँ तित श्याममयी है। (Surdasa)

Surdasa says, 'Wherever I look, I see only Shri Krishna.'

When this unique state comes to you, you will realise the authenticity of my words and the unique, special bliss inherent in the state of separation. Thus, you must enhance and increase the sentiment 'He alone is mine', and you must move forward with a spirit of service. I am the lover, and He is the Beloved. This sentiment must be strengthened.

7

The Lover

VARIOUS SUBJECTS HAVE BEEN discussed so far, but the most important is that the person who loves is the *premi*, lover, and the object of their love, *premaspada* or beloved, is either God or a Saint. Now who is it that must practise love or devotion?

People generally say that it is the soul or 'me' that practises devotion. However, the soul is inactive; it does nothing. The actual doer of all our activities is the mind. Doing mere physical work using the senses will not suffice. Activities for engaging the senses, such as *sankirtana*, etc., are done to assist you in infusing your mind quickly with God. You might say that something is better than nothing. But without the mind's attachment to God, what you are doing cannot be called *sadhana*. This is the challenge of Veda Vyasa, who says:

चेत: खल्वस्य बन्धाय मुक्तये चात्मनो मतम्। (*Bhagavatam* 3.25.15)

The mind alone is the cause of bondage and liberation.

Both take place because of the mind. So who must love? It is the mind. The lover must love the Beloved by fixing his mind on Him.

Theories Prevalent in the World

There are a lot of people who say, 'Why get involved in this business of fixing the mind on God?' There have been many supposedly great intellectuals in this world with either no intellectual capacity or limited intellectual capacity who have espoused all kinds of theories. Let us take a moment now to listen to some of them.

Sigmund Freud

There is a Western philosopher called Sigmund Freud who claimed that it is an inflexible law of nature that the human mind remains distressed. Therefore, no one should hope or endeavour for peace and happiness. Our world has produced such capable men! There is a book called *The Sickness of Civilization* in which Dr Radhakamal Mukerjee refutes Freud's theory that every person is doomed to remain distressed, restless and unfulfilled, and that this is some rigid natural law.

Arthur Schopenhauer

Another great philosopher, Arthur Schopenhauer, says that the human mind must remain swaying in restlessness and grief, and that there is no cure for it! Well, we have a cure here in India. All these people have accepted defeat because they only use their minds to think of solutions. They refuse to engage in any spiritual research, nor do they accept the views of the great sages and transcendentalists who have conducted such research. Nevertheless, they jot down their short-sighted views and call them philosophical treatises. In truth, however, all of this is nothing but the limited views of material intellects bound by *maya*.

Bertrand Russell

Bertrand Russell states that the dissatisfaction and troubles of the mind, along with its constant fluctuations, must be borne by the individual; there is no solution. However, if one engages himself in work, day and night, he can at least forget his miseries for some time. This was his prescribed method. What Russell says is mostly true because an idle mind is the devil's workshop, and so the fellow has at least suggested something practical for people to do to avoid the problem. It is during times of idleness that we think of gambling, going to clubs, watching movies, going to friends' houses to engage in criticism and praise, and various other nonsense. Whatever our mind is attached to, that is where it will run to in our spare time. And if it does not run away anywhere, then when we are sitting idly, it will engage in attachment and aversion. It is important for you to pay attention to every word. You can see that Russell's suggestion is at least helpful for common people, but it is no genuine solution.

The Uncontrollable

Sage Patanjali

The Hatha Yogis[1] say that you should wilfully control your mind. Our Darshana Shastras also describe this. This is a spiritual philosophy, not a material one. Thus, we have left the realm of materialism and have come to spirituality. Pay close attention. There is a philosophical treatise written by Sage Patanjali that deals with yoga, the method of controlling the mind. Nowadays, this word yoga is heard a lot throughout our cities, but it refers to a physical drill only. The original definition of yoga as given by Patanjali is:

योगश्चित्तवृत्तिनिरोध: ॥ (*Yoga Darshana* 1.2)

This *sutra* states that checking or controlling the tendencies or wavering of the mind is called yoga. The asanas of yoga only constitute the various physical postures that can aid in this. Yoga refers to gaining control of the mind. Patanjali outlines various techniques, which you can read about in his treatises. But in the end, even he concedes that the techniques he suggests are very difficult to implement, and even if someone does master them, there is still no guarantee that the mind will always remain in control. Things can and do go wrong, don't they? In the end, therefore, he wrote this *sutra*:

ईश्वरप्रणिधानाद्वा। (*Yoga Darshana* 1.23)

Take the shelter of God if you want definite results.

Only then will your mind come under control; otherwise, it will be controlled for only a short while and then there will be trouble. Sage Patanjali himself admitted this!

Diogenes

The West has had its fair share of Hatha Yogis too, like Diogenes, who used to beg before a stone statue for food and clothing. When he was asked why, he explained, 'I am practising tolerance, for I know that this stone figure cannot give me anything. Thus, when I approach a person and he ignores me or gives me nothing, I will not feel anything.' This was his method. But even this will not take you to the goal.

Swami Rama Tirtha

He had such a great attraction for apples. If you think about it, everybody has an attachment to something, whether big or small, good or bad. Someone likes rasagulla, someone else likes eggplant or some other vegetable. Everybody has their own likes and dislikes, their own habits.

Swami Rama Tirtha's weakness was apples. He thought, 'Every time I try to take this mind to God, it rushes to apples instead.' He sat down in front of an apple and looked at it continuously for one, two, three, seven days! The apple rotted and became infested with worms. He then propositioned his mind, 'Are you ready to eat this now?' Why is he doing all this? It is a vain attempt to control his mind by not eating an apple that he puts in front of himself. This is no solution, but an exercise in excessive stubbornness. Today you win and tomorrow, when you come across another apple, you eat it. This is no permanent cure either.

All these solutions offer temporary relief for those people who do not want to practise devotion. In truth, it is utterly impossible to control the mind in this way.

The Unstoppable

Now try to understand this in a simple way. A cyclist must keep moving either to the left or to the right or in any direction. He knows that if he stops pedalling, he will fall. In the same manner, this mind is constantly on the move, be it in this world or in God's. But either way, it cannot remain static. It is in a state of constant motion. God has given you such a machine that cannot be locked away. If you locked it, you would not be able to think, speak or move. If chloroform is applied to someone as an anaesthetic, the result is that he will fall into deep sleep, in which he will not think, see or hear.

Some of you who fall asleep here in the hall cannot hear six or seven drums beating! And if I ask such a person to stand up, they look behind as if I am addressing someone else. Sleep is such an intoxication that you remember nothing. When you finally open your eyes after a short while, you think, 'I was not sleeping; I am looking straight ahead.'[2] It is true that you are not sleeping right now, but you were four seconds ago. But you do not realise it. Thus, the mind stops altogether in deep sleep, and you do not think, understand or speak. But the mind cannot be locked anywhere permanently. To attempt to do so is unnatural. Today's psychiatrists admit this fact too.

The Unconquerable

William James

There was a renowned psychologist called William James who devised a formula, which is somewhat correct. He said there are two things – desires and well-being. If your desires are reduced and your gain is increased, then you will derive more happiness and experience a sense of greater well-being. However, if your desires are more and your gain is less, then you are headed for unhappiness and a decline in your general well-being. Accordingly, if you want happiness, reduce your cravings to zero, and if you want to increase your suffering, then increase your desires so that when your gain comes to zero, you will experience the greatest unhappiness.

What James is advocating is only theoretical. How do you reduce your longings or desires to zero? James, unfortunately, neglected explaining this in his book. What if you think, 'I will not crave anything; I will not desire anything.' If thinking could rid us of our faults, then everything would have been simple. Why would great yogis and ascetics perform such rigorous penance and practise so much discipline? This will never work because the root cause of all desire is *maya*, and until God removes it, no one can bring desires to an end.

Great sages, ascetics and yogis who could travel through the air at will, could acquire thousands of bodies simultaneously and had many other mystic powers, have not been able to control their minds. So how can you? Just to constantly say or think 'I should not increase my desires' as propagated by psychology is a very ordinary cure indeed. It is not just psychologists; everyone knows that desires are bad, but merely knowing that will not benefit you in the least. Right from the time when a child is very young, he hears his mother and father saying that lying is bad. Throughout his lifetime, he hears it infinite times, reads it infinite times, lectures others about it infinite times and then dies. But he himself is never able to give up lying. Why? Because he achieves his ends through lying. He has an attachment to worldly things

and to attain them he has to do whatever is necessary –
even lie. Just knowing it, hearing it, reading about it and
reflecting on it does not work. Therefore, this view is also
proven to be unacceptable. Granted, however, it does
have some benefits, but only to a limited degree.

David Hume

Another philosopher, David Hume, wrote in his book
that all the psychiatrists in the world, using all the various
medicines available at their disposal, cannot give a patient
the same level of relief that he experiences by following the
most ordinary and basic religious principles. He used the
word 'ordinary' – think, then, of the impact of the more
advanced religions! There are many views on the mind,
both in India and abroad, but there are no cures.

Control Is Not the Answer

The first point to note is that you will not attain ultimate
bliss through adopting any of these techniques. Pay
close attention. The substance called bliss – the divine
happiness that the soul is constantly seeking – cannot be
attained through any one of these so-called cures, even if
the impossible is achieved and desires do come to an end.
At the very most (even though it is impossible), if anger,
lust, greed, infatuation and envy do come to an end, you
will still not attain bliss. Besides, no one can bring these
mental diseases under control permanently. This is another
irrefutable fact. Therefore, we can only suppress them
temporarily. Right now, for example, all of you are free from
lust, anger and greed, and are listening to what I am saying

attentively.[3] Who would ever guess that you are afflicted by any of these maladies? But they are there within all of you, and finding the right opportunity, they will manifest themselves. If someone bumps into you, you flare up. 'Can't you see where you are going?' Anger has manifested. You see a 100-rupee note and there is no one around. You slip it into your pocket. Greed has manifested. Who is going to announce among the *satsangis*, 'Has anyone lost ₹100?' Now if it was a one-rupee note, then it gets announced because one's dignity is preserved by doing so, and the person is even termed honest by everyone else.

All bad qualities reside within us like a seed and, finding the appropriate atmosphere, manifest externally. All the various remedies discussed here only provide temporary relief and are therefore not sensible. If you are going to make the effort, then make sure that the disease is permanently cured at the root itself. I cannot go into detail about all these remedies now as it will take too long. *Nyaya, Mimansa, Vaisheshika, Yoga* by Sage Patanjali, *Vedanta* by Jagadguru Shankaracharya, and the other schools of philosophy — Nyaya, Mimansa, Vaisheshika — all describe at length how to control the mind; just understand in brief that the mind cannot be controlled.

Surrender: The Only Way

All the diseases of *maya*, like lust, anger, and so on, will not leave you until you are liberated from *maya*. And you can be liberated from *maya* only by completely surrendering to God to receive His grace. *Only through God's grace can you be liberated from maya.* It cannot take place on the foundation of any spiritual discipline.

There is only one spiritual discipline and that is surrender to God. That is all. Now what does surrender mean? 'I cannot do anything.' You must have heard, seen or read the definition of surrender. When an army at war surrenders to the enemy, it puts down its weapons and all the soldiers raise their hands in the air. If any of them hesitate or put their hands in their pockets instead of in the air, they risk getting shot. Remember this: should someone ever confront you carrying a loaded gun, just raise your hands in the air. If you do anything else, you could get yourself shot, even though you may have no concealed weapon that your assailant assumes you were reaching for. Surrender, therefore, means doing nothing. This is all that must be done to receive God's grace. All the *sadhana* we have done through many ages is simply to bring us to the state of surrender. And it is the mind that must surrender. To date, however, the mind has been surrendered to the world for infinite lives. Its prolonged practice of this makes it go round and round in circles. I explained earlier the science behind the workings of the mind and the intellect.

Your Mind, the Lover

A brief recap: what we need to pay attention to always is that the main worker behind everything is this mind. When you do any work in the world, you must pay careful attention to not allow your mind to get attached to the work. Conversely, when you engage in *sadhana*, you must make sure that your mind is attached to the divine realm. In fact, you must be careful in both cases and keep a watch on your mind. Any attachment shown in the world should be merely an act, but with the Guru and God, it must be genuine. If your mind is attached to the world and you are merely acting in the spiritual area, you will get the result of the material world and will not attain God. Even in the world, an act is not taken too seriously. In India, for example, abuse of the in-laws is done in jest during marriage ceremonies. Various liberties are taken during the festivities of Holi. No one takes them seriously. The same is also true with April Fools' Day. Hence, even the world gives no real value to acting.

The lover is therefore the mind of the individual. You can call a human being a composite of the body, soul, mind, intellect and senses. But in truth, neither does the body work, nor the senses, nor the soul. It is the work of the mind and the intellect, the *antahkarana*, that is counted. Pay close attention to this.

How to Love

Now let us move on. We must love God and His lovers, His associates, the Saints. There is a condition to love Him. What does this mean? Is there any condition in love? Yes. This is because you have never loved; you do not know how to love. How can that be? You have loved infinite fathers, mothers, husbands, and wives in infinite lifetimes. You must have had at least one in each life. Yes, but you can write it down in gold letters that you did not love any one of them, whether you were playing the epitome of lovers – Laila and Majnu, Shirin and Farhad or Romeo and Juliet. You have always loved only yourself. Only yourself!

Every soul loves only for its self-interest until the attainment of God. Every action until then is aimed towards meeting his or her own needs only. Not also — only! And what happens when one attains God? One's selfish interest in infinite and eternal happiness is attained for eternity. Now there is no reason for any more action. The very purpose behind it has been achieved. He has done what needed to be done.

The Actions of Saints

All these Saints we hear about did great work and performed all kinds of actions after attaining God. Prahlada ruled a kingdom, married, fathered children and fought battles. Similarly, Arjuna, Hanumana, Bharata and Lakshmana all performed various deeds. In fact, 99.9 per cent of Saints have. You may ask why they are performing actions. Haven't they attained what is to be achieved from all actions, that is, bliss? Yes, they have. Then their actions should have also come to an end.

For example, when you heat butter in a pan, it makes a loud sound. As the butter cooks, the impurities disperse and the frequency of the sound lowers and becomes more widely spaced until finally that butter becomes ghee. Now it is cooked and therefore silent. That ghee will not make any sound unless something is put in it to fry. Why does it make a sound? It does not make any sound for itself but because of something else which is cooking in it. When that added item is cooked, it stops making a sound. Then another item is added and the sound resumes, only stopping again after it is cooked.

In the same manner, the Saint and God, who are divine and possess divine bliss, perform actions only for the benefit of others. Just as a person under *maya* acts only for himself, the Saint and God act only for others. They are helpless in this regard and can do nothing for themselves. When there is nothing left to be done, what can these poor souls do? Just as it is impossible for us to do anything for others until we have attained divine bliss, it is impossible for God and the Saints to do anything for themselves, because they have attained bliss. They have no personal motive left.

Love Silences Distractions

God and the Saints descend to this world. Acting like worldly people, they live among us in disguise, hiding their true personality. Despite opposition, they try to help people by bringing them over to their side, and in the process, they meet with resistance from all corners. If one member of a worldly family starts moving in the direction of God, the entire clan unites to try and prevent him from becoming a devotee. 'Who is this Saint who has come to destroy our family?' It's just like it is in politics, where people unite to draw someone into their party. And the poor Saint is all alone on one side while there are millions of worldly people on the other, trying to pull back the soul that has started its spiritual life. Most succumb to this pressure and give in: 'I think I should stay with the majority.'

And those who stay on the path of devotion say:

कोउ कहौ कुलटा, कुलीन-अकुलीन कहो,
कोउ कहौ रंकिनी कलंकिनी कुनारी हौं।
कैसो नरलोक परलोक बड़लोकन में,
लीन्ही मैं अलीक लीक-लोकन ते न्यारी हौं।
तन जाहु मन जाहु देव गुरु जन जाहु,
प्रान किन जाहु टेर टरत न टारी हौं।
वृन्दावन वारी बनवारी की मुकुटवारी,
पीतपटवारी वही मूरति पै वारी हौं। (Mirabai)

I no longer care about what society says. Whether people praise or criticise me, it makes no difference. I am not concerned about this world or the next, nor about public opinion. Having chosen Krishna, I have separated myself from worldly concerns. Even if I lose my body, wealth or relationships, I will never give up my connection with Krishna. I belong fully to Him – to the Krishna of Vrindavan who wears a peacock feather and yellow robes. Seeing His divine form, I have surrendered everything.

One who determines to stay says:

घर तजौं वन तजौं नागर नगर तजौं,
वंशीवट तट तजौं काहू पै न लजिहौं।
गेह तजौं देह तजौं नेह कहौ कैसे तजौं,
काज आज राज बीच ऐसे साज सजिहौं।
बावरो भयो है लोक बावरी कहत मो को,
बावरी कहे पे हम काहू न बरजिहौं।
कहैया औ सुनैया तजौं बाप और भैया तजौं,
दैया तजौं मैया पै कन्हैया नाहिं तजिहौं। (Surdasa)

I give up the house, the forest, the city and all its inhabitants. I have no shame in singing the glories of my Beloved. I can abandon my body and my home, but how can I give up my

Beloved? The world calls me mad, but I do not argue with them. I say they are perfectly right. I have given up hearing and speaking. I have abandoned my father and brother, my mother and everyone else, but I cannot give up my Beloved Shri Krishna.

Those who persist in this way will eventually gain freedom from *maya*. This explains why it happens to a few select souls only; so few, in fact, that they can be counted on your fingers: Tulsidasa, Surdasa, Mira, Kabira, Nanaka and Tukarama. Meanwhile, the rest of the world looks on. 'Oh, he is gone. So be it. That is just one. Let us make sure no one else leaves. Let us be on guard.' God and the Saints come, armed with infinite power, but fail before people like us.

The way we apply our intellect and question everything with our innumerable ifs, buts and whys prevents us from surrendering. And without surrender, even the greatest descension of God and the foremost of Saints cannot give us anything.

God's Only Condition

There is an eternal law of giving only to surrendered souls; therefore, they cannot do anything. And if we surrender, it is only to some limited degree. What is required is one hundred per cent surrender. Even 99.99 per cent will not do.

यदा ह्येवैष एतस्मिन्नुदरमन्तरं कुरुते। (*Taittiriya Upanishad* 2.7)

The *Veda*s declare that even the slightest gap, like a hair's breadth, between you and God is unacceptable, meaning there should not be even the slightest lack in one's surrender to God. Complete and unwavering surrender is essential. Surrender must be absolute and complete. Even if you wrap a touchstone in the finest possible cloth and then touch it to some iron, the iron will not turn into gold.

What else does the *Gita* contain? In the first chapter, Arjuna says, 'I am surrendered to You.' And in the last chapter, Shri Krishna says, 'Listen to something most confidential, surrender to Me alone.'

But right at the beginning Arjuna says, 'I am surrendered to You.'

शिष्यस्तेऽहं शाधि मां त्वां प्रपन्नम्। (*Gita* 2.7)

In the beginning, Arjuna surrendered to God *also*. Now Shri Krishna is saying, 'Surrender to Me *alone*.' Herein lies the whole problem. Partial surrender will not suffice. I need hundred per cent surrender. This complete surrender means doing nothing. Since eternity, we have practised doing everything and that is why there is a lot to be done to come to this state of doing nothing. The process to reach this state has been given different names by the Saints, including *sadhana, bhajan, kirtan, upasana,* etc.

येन केन प्रकारेण मन: कृष्णो निवेशयेत्। (*Bhakti Rasamrita Sindhu*)

The mind should be attached to Shri Krishna in any way possible.

We must love Him. This is the condition. Since eternity, we have never learned how to love, so we must now learn.

8

How to Love God

YOU HAVE BEEN TOLD that the primary component in loving the Beloved is the mind. It is the mind alone which must love. You already know what it means to love, even though you do not know how to love correctly. Currently, you love for your own self-interest, and now you must learn to love for the sake of the Beloved. You just need to add this one thing to the knowledge you already have about this.

You love the world for the sake of worldly objects, so now you must love your divine Beloved for the sake of something divine. Pay close attention to both these sentences. Our past practice has been to love worldly objects for the sake of worldly needs. Now for the sake of divine love, we must love our divine Beloved and nothing else. Otherwise, our love remains the same as worldly love. There are just two new conditions:

1. Loving for a spiritual end
2. The love be directed towards a spiritual personality, our divine Beloved

Why should we have a spiritual aim? The straightforward answer to this is that we are spiritual beings. We are not this body, but the soul. If we had been the body, then it would have been all right to love material objects. But we are divine – a part of God – and therefore we cannot attain our happiness from the acquisition of any material thing. What do we mean by 'our'? That which belongs to us or the soul. This body is not us, but ours.

You say, 'Today, so-and-so left the world. A crowd of people came to pay their respects.' This is the body, a corpse. The soul has already left. This corpse was present beforehand, but because the soul was present within it, you referred to it as a live body. But as soon as the soul departs, you refer to that body as a corpse. It is made of five material elements, all of which are inert. The combination of these elements comprises the body.

The Amazing World

All the objects of the universe are merely different combinations of earth, water, fire, air and ether, and your body is one of them. There are different varieties of bodies in existence, too. The human body is unique, even the bodies of animals, birds and so on, are different and distinct from one another. You can see this with your own eyes. We do not concern ourselves with who made all this and why. Nevertheless, someone has made these various types of bodies and provided all the appropriate arrangements to go with them.

Some living beings, for example, can live only in water and cannot survive outside it. Others who can survive only outside water cannot live in water, while others can live both inside and outside water! This world is so extraordinary that to date no one has been able to give a complete definition of a single blade of grass.

The greatest intellects of infinite universes have invested a huge amount of time and energy in trying to unravel the reason or ultimate source behind creation and its maker, but to no avail. It remains unknown. And yet the world was created with each feature more astonishing than the next. Can anyone replicate it? No one to date has been able to recreate even a strand of hair on someone's head, let alone anything else. It is completely beyond the scope of any material scientist.

For example, just see how colourful a flower is. How did this flower come to be? Did someone make it? A seed was put into the earth, which grew into a tree all on its own. Did any scientist contribute to it? No. The tree came to be by itself – trunk, branches, leaves, flowers and fruit all came to be by themselves. No government was involved. Without any effort, this miracle took place. Isn't it astonishing?

In comparison, a single aeroplane that takes thousands of factory workers to construct can still fail. Being a man-made machine, mistakes can take place in manufacturing. And yet, without any government and any visible creator, this entire creation came to be and is manifesting before our eyes daily. Trees dry out and wither in the heat of the summer. The forests look barren and large areas of vegetation become desolate. Then, with the sudden arrival of rain, everything once again becomes verdant without any human involvement, such as someone going there and organising everything. You have witnessed such miracles in the world, even if only to a small extent.

What would you know of the astonishing things that happen in the infinite universes? All of this is just a play of the five elements.

The Play of God

The *Brahma Sutra* calls it a play.

लोकवत्तु लीलाकैवल्यम्। (Brahma Sutra 2.1.33)

This is the play of God. There is no effort involved in play. This is all mere child's play for God; a joke that is far beyond the combined intellects of the greatest minds in the infinite universes. It is that type of play and it is of the five material elements: not His direct play. To witness His direct play, you will have to do as I say. You will have to love Him. Then you will be able to see His direct play.

This play of the material elements has great benefits associated with it, while at the same time, it can cause great harm. There is sensible gain from it because no one can survive without it. Take trees, for example. If all the trees in the world were felled, everyone would die, regardless of whether there was enough grain and fruit to eat. Without oxygen, the whole world would come to an end.

The whole world has been created so scientifically, solely for the maintenance of the body, because it is through this body that we can perform our *sadhana* in order to surrender to God and to attain Him, which is ultimately what we are here to do. We must therefore maintain the body for this reason and do it carefully. I have told you many times that if you are careless in this regard, you will lose the very means that is your pathway to *sadhana*.

नात्यश्नतस्तु योगोऽस्ति न चैकान्तमनश्नतः। (Gita 6.16)
युक्ताहारविहारस्य युक्तचेष्टस्य कर्मसु।
युक्तस्वप्नावबोधस्य योगो भवति दुःखहा॥ (Gita 6.17)

Here, Lord Krishna emphasises balance and discipline in life for a spiritual aspirant. Eating, drinking and sleeping must be done in moderation, according to the regulations of scriptures. Just because the world has been given to you does not mean that you use it whimsically.

For example, to write something, you require a pen, some paper, your hand, your eyes and your intellect. Children write their examination papers, and you do various kinds of office work. Now if one of the above goes awry, your writing becomes useless, and you can even receive punishment. A woman cooks food using many different ingredients and she must do everything exactly right. If she uses salt instead of sugar or vice versa, all her effort will go in vain. Similarly, this world has been made to be utilised properly and not to be exploited for our sensual enjoyment. It is meant to be utilised to maintain the body. Whatever is needed for the body should be used when and where needed.

It is an example of the causeless mercy of God that when you entered your mother's womb, all preparations had already been made. As newborns, we could not digest grains and, thus, milk was provided in our mother's breasts. What a wonderful arrangement this is, and without it, we would have died shortly after our birth, and the entire world would have been useless to us.

The Great Ignorance

This *mayic* play of God is vital for the upkeep of the body, and at the same time, it is also dangerous. In our ignorance, we have mistaken ourselves to be the body and wasted infinite lives in enjoying the objects of this world for the pleasure of the body. Being the soul, we naturally receive no pleasure from all this, because the soul is a spiritual entity and divine, and its subject must therefore be divine. Our ears, eyes, nose, tongue and skin are made up of the five material elements. Therefore, their subjects must naturally be substances made of these very elements. Similarly, because the soul is a part of God, its subject can only be God.

Now you must have understood that although we do love, and we also know how to love, nevertheless, we make two mistakes in this regard. Firstly, we love for worldly reasons, and secondly, our love is misdirected towards worldly persons and objects in the material world.

Our Greatest Foolishness

Those who were more intelligent did something even more foolish. They decided that happiness lies in worldly objects, but instead of asking for it from the world, they asked for it from God! 'O God! Have mercy on me, and grant me a son and grant me wealth.' You may ask why this is considered even greater foolishness. Such people have reached the goal (by acknowledging and accepting God), but then they spoil the whole thing. It is like multiplying a billion by zero. The result of multiplying anything by zero will be zero, no matter if it is by one billion or ten billion.

Suppose you have a son whom you love dearly. When your son becomes seriously ill with typhoid or pneumonia and is on the verge of death, you rush to the doctor and with tears in your eyes, you plead, 'Please save my son. You can charge whatever you like. I do not mind the cost of the treatment, be it ₹1,000 or ₹2,000, but please save his life.' Now is this love for the doctor? No, this is love for your son. If your love was for the doctor, you would not burden him with the trouble of having to cure your son. You aim to cure your son, but through the doctor. Similarly, our attachment is to the world, but through God. We pray to God for worldly pleasures. This is the biggest foolishness. In fact, there can be no foolishness greater than this.

People often cite the story of Kalidasa as being the example of the most foolish, because he cut off the very branch of a tree on which he was sitting. But I do not accept this. Granted, he would have fallen and sustained some level of injury, but that would have healed in ten days or so. The foolishness I am speaking about is so great that infinite lifetimes have passed and we have still not managed to free ourselves from our sorrows. And if you still continue to persist on this path with arrogance, you can never hope to be free from these sorrows in the future, unless and until you renounce it. To ask for the world from the world is therefore wrong, but to ask for the world from God is even greater foolishness.

Seeking the Right

I therefore told you at the very beginning to pay attention to two things. One is that what we desire should be divine, and the second is that the person we want it from should be a divine personality. No one else has it – no celestial god or goddess, human, demon or any *sattvic*, *rajasic* or *tamasic* personality. In the infinite universes, anything that is under *maya* or is a product of *maya* cannot contain the divine happiness we seek. It is not that they can have it to a small extent either. They cannot have it at all! There is no such thing as having some or a little. Remember this: 'Bliss is always infinite. It is not a limited thing.' The definition of bliss is that which is unlimited, infinite, immeasurable, divine, indescribable and eternal. Bliss is like that!

Learn the Art of Loving

Now we all know the method of loving. What happens in our love for our mother, son, wife or husband? We desire to see that person, to embrace him or her. We desire that person to satisfy all our senses, and there is a longing for him or her to be there for us always. We are always brimming with such emotions.

Saint Tulsidasa reflected at length on how to explain to worldly people how dear Lord Rama should appear to us. People questioned him about this repeatedly. It is extremely difficult to articulate because no one in the world has ever experienced true bliss, and the so-called love of this world is absolutely no comparison to it. But what was he to do? However, he would have to offer some kind of explanation and use a worldly example too, so that people could at least get an idea. To say that the feeling of pleasure that an amorous man gets from loving a desirable woman is like the feeling Tulsidasa gets from loving Lord Rama is utter madness. But because these feelings are considered an example in the world, he presented this to us.

कामिहिं नारि पियारि जिमि लोभिहिं प्रिय जिमि दाम। (Ramayana)

Just as a lustful man loves a woman, and a greedy man cherishes wealth, in the same way, one should worship Lord Rama with deep love, abandoning all worldly attachments and desires.

Divine Passion

Akbar and a Lover

Once, Emperor Akbar decided to disguise himself and go out into his kingdom to see how his subjects were living. While out, the time for daily prayer or namaz came. The emperor spread out his prayer mat on which he sat to recite the prayers along with his subjects, and as per custom, began offering namaz. Suddenly, a woman came running towards him. Anticipating a rendezvous with her lover and being absorbed in desirous thoughts of seeing and embracing him, she inadvertently ran straight across Akbar's prayer mat. The sanctity of this prayer mat is unquestioned and held in great esteem by all Muslims as a representative of the Lord Himself, and this woman ran right over it!

Seeing this, Akbar became furious. His rage had nothing to do with the fact that he was an emperor, for anything held in such reverence, when desecrated, can spark anger even in a common person. Akbar ordered that she be found and brought before his court. 'We will have to think of a punishment worse than death for her!' The death penalty is imposed on ordinary criminals, but what she did had never been done before, and it was committed so unnecessarily. When there was so much space that she could have run in, the fact that she ran over a small prayer mat was unforgivable.

Akbar got up from his prayers in a fury and the woman was captured and presented before him. 'How could you do such a thing?' The woman replied, 'Your Majesty! I would not dare commit such a crime even against an ordinary Muslim during namaz. How then could I do so against you, a great emperor?' Akbar yelled, 'Am I lying? You did it!'

The woman continued timidly, 'I am not lying, Your Majesty! I now know I can speak frankly, for it is certain that you will sentence me to death. But you see, I was in love with a worldly man and being engrossed in that love, I ran with no awareness of my surroundings. I stepped on your prayer mat without realising that I was inviting my death. How could I possibly do something so abhorrent in a normal state, knowing full well that the outcome would be facing your court and certain death?

But may I say that what is truly sorrowful in this case is that you were supposed to be totally absorbed in the worship of your divine Beloved, and yet you noticed me? Let it be known to the whole world that you did not acknowledge God, Khuda, as your emperor.'

Tears filled Akbar's eyes, and falling at her feet, he said, 'You speak the truth. I should have been absorbed in Him during prayer.' This incident gives us some insight into how absorbed a person can become, even in mundane worldly love.

It is true that such heights of love happen only sometimes and only to a select few, when the level of attachment crosses a certain limit. It cannot happen all the time. The woman who stepped on the prayer mat would have become normal again on seeing her husband, and when she sees him throughout the day at home. During these times, she will also experience feeling detached from him.

All of you are familiar with what happens after that. 'Oh, my life was ruined the day I married you!' She could also reach this point. This, however, is not a permanent state. It cannot remain the same forever because this is not love at all. In fact, there is no question of love here. There can temporarily be a sentiment wherein complete absorption takes place, provided both the man and the woman are overcome by a passionate desire for each other.

Be Greedy for God Alone

कामिहिं नारि पियारि जिमि।

Thus, Tulsidasa gave this example, 'Just as a passionate man finds a woman attractive', to give worldly people some idea, since he had no other means of explaining. Still not satisfied, he gave another example to show how intense our love for God should be.

लोभिहिं प्रिय जिमि दाम।

Just as a greedy man loves money.

You may understand love for money, but not the love of a greedy man.

Once, there was an excessively greedy merchant. He said, 'To hell with food and drink, and with the love of a wife, a son or the rest of the world! All I want is money. When will I make a million?' Once that was done, it was, 'When will I make two?' After that, 'When will I make three?' In this way, all he did was plan and practise, plan and practise. 'This person is still wealthier than I am. Now I have overtaken him. Now I have to surpass that person.' In this way, he was constantly competing unnecessarily with other wealthy people, as if caught in a never-ending horse race. Every soul harbours some degree of love for money, but a greedy man goes to such an extent that he can take out an insurance policy on his wife, kill her and get the money. He then marries again and murders for money. This sort of thing happens in this world. Everyone does all kinds of things for it. You people are familiar with all the plans and plots you make to earn money.

This greedy merchant would close his shop at night to count the money he had earned during the day. One day, his sales had been so excessive that a lot of time passed as he counted all his money. His maidservant took his food to him at the usual time, but he did not acknowledge her. It became 10 p.m., then 12 a.m., and even 1 a.m. and 2 a.m., and still he had not finished! He just could not help himself; it felt so good counting it all.

After a few failed attempts, the maidservant gave up trying to give him his meal, and so his wife went instead. 'It's going to be morning soon and your counting has not yet ended. We must endure this behaviour, this too you know!' He ignored her. To hell with his wife and the whole world. In the end, she decided to put something sweet into his mouth, thinking that the taste would break his trance. Tasting the sweet dish in his mouth, he said, 'Oh, I have finished eating,' and went over to the washbasin to wash his hands and mouth before promptly returning to his tallying. His wife was stunned. 'No one can do anything for you! Now you will give up food and drink and die in a few days.' This is an intense attachment to money.

When I go to Calcutta and Bombay, I watch the fun. People there have some love for God and for the Guru, but they cannot come for *satsanga*. Why? 'I close my shop very late at night.' So close your shop early and come. 'Oh no, that would result in a loss of ₹1,000 daily.' A greedy person experiences a special pleasure in acquiring money, and his desire is ever increasing.

These examples by Tulsidasa apply to the exceptionally passionate or extremely greedy and can be understood truly only by them, that is, having love for a woman or wealth to such a degree that you are completely absorbed in it to the exclusion of everything else. It cannot be understood even by an ordinary greedy person.

It is this state of exclusive absorption in God, our Beloved, which we must reach. We must be completely absorbed. The world should seem to be void in His separation.

शून्यायितं जगत् सर्वं गोविन्दविरहेण मे। (Gauranga Mahaprabhu)

There remains no charm for me. O my Beloved Govinda,
Your separation has made me so.

It may not happen immediately; it may take ten days, ten years or ten lives. There is no associated time limit. How quickly you reach this state depends entirely upon you. How much you surrender to God is entirely up to you. If your level of surrender is only 10 per cent, then you will receive 10 per cent benefit, and if it is 100 per cent, then your benefit will also be 100 per cent.

Let Go of Ownership

Once, a king went to Jesus and asked, 'How does one acquire the divine wealth that you possess? What do I have to do?' The king asked with great fervour, as though he expected it to be mere child's play. Jesus looked at him and said, 'Son, if you want divine wealth, then you must give away all your worldly wealth. If you want spiritual wealth in its entirety, then you must give up your entire material property. The pride that comes from the possession of a million, a kingdom, a wife, a son, a mansion, a body, and so on, has to be given up.' You must free yourself from all feelings of ownership. If you think you can do this with all of them around you, then well and good, but it is next to impossible. Only yogis can be devoid of feelings of ownership in the presence of worldly goods. It is not possible for an ordinary householder to do so. Such a person can feel the absence of this feeling of ownership only upon the complete removal of all personal possessions. You all have money in the bank, but you may not have it in your pockets. People say, 'Today I needed ₹5, and I had to ask the driver.'

Hence, sometimes even a wealthy person may not be carrying even a small amount of money with him, and in such situations, he will meet with trouble even though he has millions in his bank account. He is very proud of his wealth, although it is in the bank and he can only show it on paper. This method of attachment to worldly objects just needs to be diverted and directed to the divine realm. You do not have to learn anything new.

Constant Reflection

In worldly love, there is constant thinking and constant reflection, whether it is in response to feelings of attachment or aversion, friendship or enmity. A girl thinks about a boy: 'Yes, he is very nice. His eyes are nice, his nose is nice, his ears are nice, his manner of talking is nice, and his way of walking is nice too.' Her constant thinking and reflection result in her reaching a state of total absorption in him. The person who thinks less reaches a more mediocre level of love, while the one who wonders why they should think about it at all sits in peace.

Suppose three boys suddenly see a girl. One becomes completely infatuated with her and feels he would die without her. One feels some mild attraction for her and the third says, 'What is there to get so attached over? There are thousands of girls. Why are you so crazy about this one? How will you live in the world? If you want to achieve anything, either in this world or the next, you need to maintain your equilibrium. If you get married, then you will get attached, but to just get attached to any girl that comes along is not the intelligence of a human.'

Look at this! One boy is giving a lecture to the boy who is infatuated with the girl. In response, the one who has constantly thought of her says, 'What do you know about all this? I cannot get her out of my head just like that, you know!' What is so special about her that he cannot stop thinking about her? He has forced her in there with his constant thinking!

ध्यायतो विषयान्पुंस: सङ्गस्तेषूपजायते।
सङ्गात्सञ्जायते काम: कामात्क्रोधोऽभिजायते॥
क्रोधाद्भवति सम्मोह: सम्मोहात्स्मृतिविभ्रम:।
स्मृतिभ्रंशाद् बुद्धिनाशो बुद्धिनाशात्प्रणश्यति॥ (*Gita* 2.62, 2.63)

When a person keeps thinking about sense objects,
attachment to them develops. From attachment comes desire,
and from unfulfilled desire arises anger. From anger comes
confusion; from confusion, loss of memory. When memory
is lost, intelligence is destroyed. And when intelligence is
lost, one falls from the spiritual path.

This is the link. You become attached to that object which your mind again and again ascribes as happiness.

विषयान् ध्यायतश्चित्तं विषयेषु विषज्जते।
मामनुस्मरतश्चित्तं मय्येव प्रविलीयते॥ (*Bhagavatam* 11.14.27)

This verse emphasises that pure, unwavering devotion (*bhakti*) to the Supreme Lord cannot arise in the heart until one has let go of worldly attachments and impurities (like lust, anger, greed). Once those impurities are shed, the mind naturally loses interest in material pleasures and becomes inclined towards divine love.

Therefore, Veda Vyasa says that worldly objects, such as wine, meat, tea or cigarettes, or inert objects capture the mind completely because of constant thinking and revision, causing you to reach a point where you cannot have peace without it and become addicted. When these inert objects can capture your mind, imagine if you constantly thought of the divine and experienced the higher bliss inherent in it just once. Then, no one could remove that from your mind.

Therefore, to love worldly people or objects for worldly reasons must be completely renounced. Moreover, to love God or Guru for worldly reasons and to surrender to them over those reasons is even more dangerous. Therefore, we must give up both.

9

Desires and Love

YOU HAVE BEEN TOLD that to desire the world from worldly people is foolish and to desire the world from God is even greater foolishness. We should first love God, and only then should we ask Him for something. Even in the world, we only ask from those whom we love, with whom we have a close relationship, and not just anyone and everyone. We love the world and not God, yet to ask anything from someone whom we do not love would be a joke. Do not ever do this, even by mistake. Now let us move on.

Ramakrishna Paramahamsa

You all must have heard that Ramakrishna Paramahamsa developed cancer of the throat. Even today, there is no definitive cure for cancer anywhere in the world, so there was no question of a cure during his lifetime. Everyone knew that his death was imminent. By this time, he had gained great renown throughout Calcutta and Bengal as a Saint who had healed many individuals. People went to him and said, 'You have attained perfection. To rid yourself of cancer is mere child's play for you. All you have to do is request the Divine Mother and the cancer will be cured instantly.' Just think, what is cancer to someone capable of removing *maya*?

However, Ramakrishna Paramahamsa's reply was a stern one: 'You expect me to take my mind, which I have immersed in the Divine Mother, away from Her and put it on my cancer? I have loved Her to acquire Her service. How can I now ask Her for such a dirty thing? I cannot engage in such pettiness and ask for Her help for this wretched body. It is a good thing that cancer has come. Even if I am cured, I will still have to leave my body at the appointed time. It could be for another reason, like heart failure.' He further said, 'Everyone must leave at their scheduled time. Besides, what objection do I have to this hole in my throat? This body already has nine holes – the eyes, nose, ears, and so on. What is so special if I have a tenth that I should bother the Divine Mother about it? No, it would be very wrong of me to do so.' Everyone, whether a sage, ascetic, yogi, Saint or even God Himself, must leave at the appointed time. Even God does not stay a moment longer than the pre-planned period of His descension, let alone anyone else.

Lord Rama

You must have heard of an incident in Ayodhya in connection with this. Yamaraja, the god of death, came to Lord Rama to inform Him that His descension period was over. Of course, Yamaraja approaches God and the Saints reverently, placing his head at their feet before informing them, 'My Lord! I have come to fulfil my duty by telling You that your time on Earth is up. However, You may choose to stay or leave as You wish.'

It is true that, as per universal law, Yamaraja has to approach God and the Saints to inform or remind them that their time is up, but Yamaraja cannot force God or the Saint to leave as he can with everyone else. Nevertheless, the supremely independent Lord Rama did not stay a moment longer than His scheduled 11,000 years. At the exact time, to the exact second, He disappeared.

This is true of every descension of God and every Saint – Tulsidasa, Surdasa, Mira, Kabira. When God, the maker of this rule, never breaches it, why would a Saint, who is, after all, a servant of God? When someone says that they do not want to die, there can be two probable reasons – one sensible and the other foolish. The foolish reason is when the person about to die is so attached to the world – to their wealth, home, father, mother, wife and son – that they yearn to see them and embrace them one more time, and so they do not want to leave. In contrast, a *sadhaka* who has reached a high level in his devotional practice laments, 'Oh! I have not yet attained God. If I just had a little more time, I could achieve my goal.' This is like when children have their examinations and discover that there is a gap of four days between them. They feel elated because they will have four more days to prepare for the final examination. But God and the Saints have nothing to attain, and therefore, they leave at the appointed time without the slightest trace of reluctance.

The Cause of One's Downfall

In this way, to ask God for the world is the greatest foolishness and should not be done even after attaining love for Him. I have explained all this in detail in *Prema Rasa Siddhanta*.[1] Read it. It explains the various reasons why you should not ask God for anything, no matter how great the material object may be.

यत्पृथिव्यां व्रीहियवं हिरण्यं पशव: स्त्रिय:।
न दुह्यन्ति मन:प्रीतिं पुंस: कामहतस्य ते॥ (*Bhagavatam* 9.19.13)
नालमेकस्य पर्याप्तं तस्मात्तृष्णां परित्यजेत्। (*Vishnu Purana* 4.10.24)

Even if you were granted lordship over infinite universes, your desires would not be reduced even by 0.1 per cent. All your cravings and yearnings would continue unabated. As a matter of fact, they would become stronger upon receiving the object of your longing.

Sage Saubhari

There was a great sage known as Saubhari. He is mentioned in the *Rigveda*, in which there is a *Saubhari Sutra*. There is also the *Saubhari Samhita*, which is a separate text altogether. He is therefore no ordinary sage, but one who has been mentioned in the *Vedas*. You must have heard of the snake, Kaliya, who was expelled by Shri Krishna from the Yamuna River. Once, Garuda swooped down from the sky and tried to eat Kaliya, but Saubhari prevented him from doing so by saying that he was now in his shelter, and so Garuda had to return to wherever he had come from. You can see from this the heights of his power, and he used it to practise his spiritual discipline under the river Yamuna. However, one day, due to an unfortunate moment of bad association (that is commonplace in the world), he saw two fish mating and the desire arose in his mind for intimacy with a woman. He abandoned his meditational trance and came out of the water, wondering where to go to fulfil his desire.

There was a famous king in Ayodhya at the time called Mandhata, who had 50 daughters, each more beautiful than the other, possessing all good qualities and proficient in all the arts. Saubhari went to him, thinking that since he had 50 daughters, he would surely be willing to give him one in marriage. You see, Saubhari was not willing to marry just any ordinary woman. He presented his plea before the king, who thought to himself, 'Why does this 1,000-year-old man want to get married?' But Saubhari was no ordinary sage; he was renowned. Even celestial gods feared him, and King Mandhata was frightened of being cursed if he did not comply with his request. But at the same time, he wondered, 'Which girl's life shall I ruin by giving her away to this decrepit old man?' Finally, the king resolved, 'I have no objection. You sit here and I will bring all my 50 daughters to stand in front of you. The one that chooses you will be yours to marry.' King Mandhata knew that none of his princesses would choose Saubhari and so he would be saved in the process from any curse. But Saubhari saw through the king's cunning plan, so he returned the next day after transforming himself by using his yogic powers into an extremely handsome and dashing young man. Seeing him, every princess wanted to marry him, and so Saubhari married all 50 of them!

The king was again concerned, this time about the probability of fighting among his 50 daughters, each vying for the attention of her husband. Saubhari understood this too, and so, using his yogic powers, he assumed 50 bodies and created 50 palaces, one for each wife. He then fathered ten sons with each of them, and those sons in turn had ten sons of their own, and then great-grandchildren soon followed, and in this way, thousands of years passed.

One day, Saubhari came to his senses and stated:

अहो इमं पश्यत मे विनाशम् (*Bhagavatam* 9.6.50)

O humans! Observe my downfall. Look at where I was and where my desire to enjoy the world has taken me. Those of you who are making plans to enjoy the opulence of this world, take heed. I have experienced everything. You will never be able to surpass me. Your youth will last a meagre ten to fifteen years, after which the afflictions of old age will start affecting you. I, on the other hand, created a superior body through yogic power and lived with fifty women for thousands of years. But look at the depths of my downfall. Be warned! Do not venture in this direction.

Worldly opulence, however great it may be, cannot provide happiness. Leave aside fifty wives, in the *Bhagavatam* (canto 6, chapters 14–15),[2] we have the story of Chitraketu, who had ten million wives, a son and wealth to an extreme limit, and yet the family repented when they came to their senses and declared, 'We have had the experience. Please understand that there is danger lurking here.' To ask for the world from the world is therefore foolishness, but to ask for the world from God is even greater foolishness.

Beyond *Maya*

Now let us go beyond these two. The realm of love begins beyond these two. What we have spoken about so far are the two conditions of people devoted to the material world. Now let us look at those who practise devotion to that which is beyond *maya*.

Here, there are three classes. The first category is called *samartha rati*, who are completely selfless. The second is *samanjasa rati*, which is a mixture of self-interest and selflessness. The third class is called *sadharani rati*, which only has selfish desires. Note that all three are Saints and are therefore beyond *maya*, because their minds are fully surrendered and attached to Shri Krishna. But this has been done in three separate ways.

If iron is gently brought into contact with a touchstone, by chance or in a fit of rage, the iron will turn into gold, no matter what way the contact has been made.

कामं क्रोधं भयं स्नेहमैक्यं सौहृदमेव च।
नित्यं हरौ विदधतो यान्ति तन्मयतां हि ते॥ (*Bhagavatam* 10.29.15)

Similarly, if our mind gets attached to God with any sentiment – lust, anger or fear – we will go beyond *maya* and attain His abode for all eternity.

Selfish Love

Sadharani Rati

Now a lot of people, I would say 99 per cent, think that *sakama bhakti*, devotion with desires, means to worship God and ask for the world. This is not *sakama bhakti*. As a matter of fact, this is not devotion at all! You can call it devotion to the world instead.

Devotion with desires is devotion in which all desires of the senses are related to God alone, but for one's own happiness. Pay careful attention to each word. The one who, for his own happiness, desires the satisfaction of all his senses from God alone can be called a *sakama bhakta*, a devotee with desires. His eyes crave to see only God, his ears only want to hear His sweet words, his nose hankers for His divine fragrance, his tongue desires to taste the divine nectar and his skin desires only His contact. Every pore of the devotee's body has desires related to God only, and none related to anything or anyone in the *mayic* realm. If Indra, the king of celestials, is ready to share his throne, he will say, 'I do not want it even if I had the entire throne to myself.'

Remember these three points in connection with a devotee with selfish desires, right up to the time you attain God: (1) He desires to satisfy his own senses; (2) only through Shri Krishna; and (3) for his own happiness. This is a *sakama bhakta*. He does not have even 0.1 per cent attraction for anything material. You have heard of many of them – Draupadi, Gajaraja, Kubja, etc.

There are some problems with this type of love, especially during the stage of *sadhana*. And even in the stage of perfection, such devotion will award you a third-grade result. In the world, the third class of something is not considered good. 'Did you pass your bachelor's degree?' 'Yes.' 'With what grade?' Now the person looks downcast because he has a third-grade result. However, this devotee will still attain God. His *maya* is dispelled forever and all its associated by-products that afflict everyone are therefore eliminated – the three *gunas*, the three types of *karma*, the three disorders, *tridosha*, the five afflictions, *panchaklesha*, and the five sheaths, *panchakosha*. But does this devotee see the *raas*? No. That is reserved only for the first class of devotees. A third-class devotee has no access there.

Why does God show partiality like this? Why does someone attain the *maharaas* while someone else is categorised as third class? The problem lies with the instructions given by the Guru during the stage of *sadhana*. He did not caution us and we started on the wrong path. You cannot take the road to Allahabad and reach Lucknow. You must take the road to Lucknow to reach Lucknow. The Guru who is guiding you will give you instructions according to the level he himself has attained, and you will attain that level. If you have a *sakama bhakta* as your Guru, then he will teach you that method of devotion, because his attainment was on that path, and he knows nothing beyond it.

The Silent Lurking Danger

On this path of devotion with selfish desires, there is great danger lurking in the stage of devotional practice, because God will not respond to your pleas, as He will when you attain perfection. At that stage, you demand and He gives promptly. When you attain God, whether you are a selfish or selfless devotee, you bring God under your control because you have divine love. There is no question of seeing Him face-to-face without having divine love and divine vision. This is the rule applicable to everyone. But having attained divine love, you can call Him at will, and He will have to respond immediately.

When Draupadi called Him, He came immediately. Draupadi had transcended *maya*. If she called Him again after He had incarnated as her sari, after just a few seconds, He would have come again. If she calls Him every second, He will come. He will keep coming and going at her whim, without any ifs or buts, because He is bound by her devotion, and He loves to serve His devotees.

But, if a *sadhaka* at the devotional stage, who has not surrendered completely, gets into some trouble and calls Shri Krishna for help and He does not come, he could lose faith. Draupadi was fully surrendered, whereas this person has not even reached the stage of 50 per cent surrender. Even in the case of Draupadi, as long as she relied on her own strength by clenching the sari between her teeth, Shri Krishna did not come, just to teach us that He will not come until the stage of complete surrender is reached.

अनन्याश्चिन्तयन्तो मां ये जना: पर्युपासते।
तेषां नित्याभियुक्तानां योगक्षेमं वहाम्यहम्॥ (*Gita* 9.22)
ये तु सर्वाणि कर्माणि मयि संन्यस्य मत्परा:।
अनन्येनैव योगेन मां ध्यायन्त उपासते॥ (*Gita* 12.6)
तेषामहं समुद्धर्ता मृत्युसंसारसागरात्। (*Gita* 12.7)

These beautiful verses from the *Gita* express the Lord's promise of complete protection and grace to those who surrender to Him with exclusive devotion.

He takes responsibility for you only upon full surrender. And you are at the stage where you cannot fulfil this condition, but you want the same results that Draupadi got. If not received, the *sadhaka* can say, 'Shri Krishna is a liar, and the entire body of scripture is also lying. I called out to Him, and that too with tears, not just calling out.' This poor soul, who is at the *sadhana* stage and performing devotion for his material desires, can get bewildered and fall into danger. He can even go to the extent of becoming an atheist. So many souls have in the past.

Many people have come to me and said, 'Maharaj Ji, an incident took place in my life and out of rage I threw the Deity of God out of my house.' One can turn into an atheist if his worldly desires are not fulfilled. Even if you do not become a declared atheist, some doubt or the other gets created in your mind. 'Maybe all these stories are an exaggeration, because I repeatedly called out to God and yet my son died.' 'I spent my entire life chanting "Radhe Radhe" but did not get a hearing of my case.'

Nourishing desires in the *sadhana* stage could therefore lead to a great downfall, and the little love that you have for God could be reduced to zero. For this reason, I am now personally and publicly declaring that it would be better to remain an atheist. Do not approach God. If you go to Him, I forbid you to go with any desire, right up to the desire for liberation. Desires are so dangerous that if they are not fulfilled, your love can reverse and you might end up taking some other path, other than the one towards the divine.

You might think, 'I love my Guru so much. I have been here for ten days, and Guru Ji has not even spoken to me.' This is your yardstick for measuring love! Love in the divine realm follows a very crooked path indeed. The scriptures say, 'The path of love is crooked like a snake.'

भगवद् रसिक रसिक की बातें,
रसिक बिना कोउ समुझि सकै ना। (*Bhagavat Rasika*)

The *Bhagavat Rasika* declares that the words and actions of a Rasika Saint can only be understood by another Rasika Saint. The intellects of Brihaspati (preceptor of gods) and Sarasvati (the goddess of knowledge and wisdom) will fail if they try to gauge the actions of the divine realm.

10

Unveiling the Saint's Love

LOVE IS OF THREE kinds. Try to comprehend this in the simplest way so that you can understand it forever. In the first kind, there is love within and it also manifests through external behaviour. The second type of love is also within, but it is not shown on the outside. The third type of love is also within, but there is contrary or unfavourable external behaviour.

This third type is child's play for God and the Saints. They take pleasure in fooling around and therefore deliberately test you just to see if your love is genuine or imperfect. They act in a contrary manner. If your love is genuine, you will smile and say, 'It is all right.'

Bhishma's Devotion

Consider Bhishma's response to Shri Krishna lifting the chariot wheel to attack him. Shri Krishna was ready to kill him, but Bhishma started laughing and said, 'Come, come. Why have You stopped? Let us see if You have the courage to come forward.' Just look at Bhishma's enemy. He, whose mere thought can destroy infinite universes, is acting like He is at the ultimate limit of fury. His teeth are clenched, His eyebrows are twisted in anger, perspiration is pouring from His body, which is drenched in blood from the wounds made by Bhishma's arrows, and yet Bhishma is laughing and thinking, 'Do this acting with someone else. I know everything. Come forward. Why have You stopped after taking a step? I know everything.'

There is love filled within for Bhishma, infinite love, and yet Shri Krishna's external behaviour is to the contrary — displaying enmity. It is this vision of external fury on the face and figure of Shri Krishna, that Bhishma meditated upon during the last six months of his life as he lay on a bed of arrows. He could not take that vision of Shri Krishna out of his mind, with His yellow garments fluttering, His eyebrows twisted in anger and His teeth clenched. It was so beautiful for him to see His acting.

The Unusual Ways of the Saints

Contrary behaviour is therefore the norm there. If they behave favourably then consider it great mercy, because Rasika Saints follow the principle of always hiding their love! And what is their method of concealment? Contrary behaviour, so that no one knows. Saints do, however, bend this rule according to the prevailing circumstances. For example, if they showed contrary behaviour during this current age of Kali, not a single soul would even start on the path towards God. Hence, they tread carefully with this, rarely showing this type of contrary behaviour and only when a soul is eligible and not before, otherwise that soul could turn away and leave. However, if you read the histories of Saints in previous ages, like Satya, Treta and Dvapara, their behaviour was such that you would say, 'Had I been there at that time, I would have never accepted them as Saints.'

The Saint and Flies

Once, a king went to a Saint. He climbed down from his elephant and, showing his respects as per the etiquette of the time, asked the Saint for some service. According to ancient customs, people with worldly possessions would make such a request to a Saint. The Saint laughed and said, 'Everything is fine here, except for the flies. Get rid of them for me.' The king said, 'That is beyond my power.' 'When even flies are not in your control, then what claim are you making of service? Go away. You are blocking the sun from me by standing in the way.' The king was dumbfounded. He had heard so much about these ascetics, and now this Saint was challenging him and addressing him in terse and dismissive words.

If the definition of service were given to you, everyone would lower their heads and say, 'Truly, I have never performed any service.' While performing service, the feeling of I am giving is there within us, but it should never arise. Moreover, if it is disclosed to someone, the purpose of your service is defeated. On the other hand, tears of joy should fill your eyes on the thought that Guru and God are accepting your services. 'O how fortunate I am!' It is so naive to think, 'I am serving them,' when we have not yet understood the real meaning of *seva*, or service.

Sage Durvasa and Shri Krishna

Sage Durvasa used to go through the streets calling out, 'Please make me a Guru. Someone become my disciple, but if you make any mistake in your service, it will not be safe for you.' This was his slogan. Now everyone knew he was a great Saint with extraordinary powers, but the condition he laid down made everyone say, 'We are better off without a Guru,' because which worldly soul can lay claim to being able to perform service without making a mistake?

Even upon hearing Durvasa's loud calls in the streets, no one was ready to become his disciple, and so he went to Dvarika, where there are multitudes of Saints. God is personally there, and all His wives are Saints, so there is no question of *maya* entering that city. But even there, when people heard his conditions, they refused to become his disciple. A messenger went to Shri Krishna and reported the arrival of Durvasa. Shri Krishna said, 'Call him. I will become his disciple.' Thus, Durvasa got one disciple.

He, who is the Guru of the world, the Jagadguru, is today going to be a disciple of Durvasa. Who else would have the courage? He kept Durvasa in His palace and assigned many expert maidservants to his service.

The first thing Durvasa asked for was kheer (rice pudding). Rukmini began to wonder, 'What type of ascetic is this? They are supposed to eat whatever they get in alms, and Durvasa is making demands right at the outset?' An ascetic would usually wait until some degree of informality is reached in a person's house before saying something like, 'My Gopal would like to eat vermicelli pudding.' On the pretext of feeding the stone deity that they carry around with them, they eat all kinds of delicacies. You might have experienced this. But all this happens when a certain degree of informality has been reached. However, Durvasa asked right at the outset, 'I want some kheer.' Thus, his desire was fulfilled. Rukmini is the descension of Mahalakshmi and there is no dearth of anything there. All the supernatural powers personified are Her maidservants.

Durvasa ate a spoonful or so and then told Shri Krishna, 'Smear this on Your body.' Rukmini started to wonder what kind of baba he was and what was wrong with her Husband, that He was listening to him and taking all this so meekly. For His part, Shri Krishna smeared the kheer over His body. He asked Rukmini to do the same. Durvasa then went to the palace he was staying in and set fire to it. All the maidservants fled. But what could anyone say when Shri Krishna himself had made him His Guru? Durvasa said, 'I want to go for a ride. Prepare a chariot, but instead of horses, I want You and Rukmini.'

Rukmini thought to herself, 'This was the only thing remaining to be done. I have to become a horse now!' Durvasa climbed onto the chariot with a whip in his hand. Rukmini, being the descension of Mahalakshmi, is famous for the delicacy and softness of Her limbs. The soles of Her feet always remain on top of lotus petals and therefore she is called Kamalasana. She started pulling the chariot, and that too barefoot, because footwear is forbidden in front of the Guru. After some time, Rukmini's shoulders began to sag. Shri Krishna remained silent, completely overwhelmed by the joy of serving His Guru.

He told Durvasa that she is not eligible to be a disciple. 'Let Me handle the chariot alone. Tell Me what speed you want and which planet you wish to go to.' Durvasa replied, 'All right! All right! You have passed the test. I do not have to go anywhere. All this contrary behaviour was just an act to test You and You have passed. But You made one mistake. I asked You to smear Your entire body with kheer, but You did not put it on the soles of Your feet. Therefore, an arrow will hit the soles of Your feet when the time for Your departure comes. This is because You did not obey my instructions completely.' This is not just some story, but a historical incident recorded in the *Vedas*.

Beyond Appearances, Look Within

Saints therefore behave in a contrary manner, and this was the case 99 per cent of the time in ancient times. However, in this age, Tulsidasa, Surdasa, Mira, Nanaka, Kabira, Tukarama and other Saints have done this only occasionally, because they have had to keep the welfare of fallen souls in mind, those who cannot tolerate or bear much.

Who knows how much philosophy they understand? Are they the sort that just nod their heads in lectures and later say, 'Sir, you spoke very well today.' Whether or not the subject was delivered well or badly is not the point. The point is whether the subject has been firmly imbibed by you after understanding it properly. If it is firmly imbibed, it should always remain with you and never be forgotten. When someone insults you, those insulting words remain in your memory. 'He told me to get out!' This rankles in your memory. In the same way, you should always remember divine knowledge and not allow it to escape from your mind.

The behaviour of a Saint is therefore not to be seen. Any favourable behaviour on his part is done out of etiquette. In his natural state, he would not bother with favourable behaviour at all. But to fulfil his mission of individuals' welfare, he somehow controls his nature. Those Saints who have not concerned themselves with the welfare of others have behaved most erratically. You can read their histories;

no one had the courage to go near them. But those Saints who have descended for the welfare of others must renounce their naturality to mingle with us. They must wear clothes to appear normal. They must learn our behaviour, our etiquette and customs and then work on taking us out of the world. The police go undercover sometimes to mingle with the criminals that they are trying to catch, even infiltrating their gangs. Saints work similarly.

You cannot imagine how difficult their work is. Even if your intelligence was multiplied infinitely, you still would not be able to comprehend the effort they have to make for us and with us, and how servile they have to become for us. We commit offences and transgressions, which, according to law, should get us expelled from a Saint's *satsanga* for a lifetime. But still the Saint fawns on us, remaining ever hopeful that we will reform in the future. Does he have any personal motive in all this? Motive! He is someone who rejects the divine abode of Vaikuntha and the association of Lord Mahavishnu and Mahalakshmi, speaking his mind to them in his own topsy-turvy language. What could he possibly gain from the souls of this world who are bound by *maya*?

But he does have a self-interest, and that is the welfare of all souls. And for that, he must humble himself and act as a servant for these souls. He forgives all their sins and remains ever hopeful that they will rectify themselves. He knows that there is no soul who will not commit transgressions before the attainment of God. There has not been a soul since eternity who has not committed spiritual transgressions.

Never Forget the Law

Therefore, do not measure the love of a Saint by observing his external behaviour. I have repeatedly explained the law that governs God and the Saints. They must love us as much as we love them and are surrendered to them. This is the law. Understand this forever. Never doubt this law and do not look at their behaviour; look at your own love instead. If your love decreases, so will theirs. 'But the relationship seems normal. He is speaking to me as usual.' That is just acting. Because you are acting with him, trying to fool Him, He is doing the same with you. He will act in the same way as you do. As much as your love is factual, so will His be. Thus, your love is the exact measure of His love. 'I serve a soul to the exact extent of his love for Me, and according to his sentiments. This is an irrefutable law.'

ये यथा मां प्रपद्यन्ते तांस्तथैव भजाम्यहम्। (*Gita* 4.11)

In this way, you must have understood that God alone is your object of love, and the desires of your senses should be connected only to Him. But if it is for your own happiness, then it is considered selfish devotion and therefore third-class. There is also the danger that if He does not appear before you or fulfil some desire of yours, then you will think He does not care for you, and so you stop caring for Him. You will then do what you have always done in your worldly relationships with your spouse, parents and children: you will turn your back on God and the Saints and even be ready to go to hell. A soul can fall to such depths. All this can happen from practising selfish devotion. Therefore, it is wrong to do so.

11

Selfless Love

YOU WERE TOLD THAT loving the world for worldly reasons is dangerous and to love God for worldly gain is wrong. The reason is that as we do not yet have love for God, the question of Him fulfilling our desires does not arise. Even if we do develop love for God and maintain desires, there are various losses we will incur.

Therefore, to have all desires of the senses only in connection with God, but for our own happiness, is called *sadharani rati, sakama bhakti* or selfish devotion. This is also not praiseworthy, because although the soul practising this type of devotion will become a Saint and be free from *maya*, he will not find a place among the Saints of a higher level.

Harmonious Love

Samanjasa Rati

Above them are the Saints who look for their own happiness and the happiness of their Beloved. There is a mixture of selflessness and selfishness in their love. A superficial version of this type of love can be seen in the world, in a husband-and-wife relationship, where both take care of each other's interests. This love is called *samanjasa rati*.

Wherever there was a husband-and-wife relationship, for example, that of Shri Krishna and Rukmini and the queens of Dvarika, there was love of the *samanjasa rati* category.

नायं श्रियोऽङ्ग उ नितान्तरतेः प्रसादः
स्वर्योषितां नलिनगन्धरुचां कुतोऽन्याः।
रासोत्सवेऽस्य भुजदण्डगृहीतकण्ठ-
लब्धाशिषां य उदगाद् व्रजवल्लवीनाम्॥ (*Bhagavatam* 10.47.60)

But you know that even the Lord's own spouse, Mahalakshmi, did not acquire the place, the seat or the nectar of bliss that the purely selfless *gopis* did. Her love was the *samanjasa rati* type, where she looked for her own happiness, along with the happiness of Shri Krishna. Therefore, even this type of love is not acceptable.

Perfectly Selfless Love

Samartha Rati

True love is only of one type. Sage Narada gives a very beautiful definition of love:

तत्सुखसुखित्वम्। (*Narada Bhakti Sutra* 24)

To remain happy in His happiness.

Remember this formula forever: remain happy in His happiness. We are His servants. This is the fact, no matter which sentiment we choose to serve in — *madhurya bhava*, *sakhya bhava* or *vatsalya bhava*. The duty of the servant is to keep his master happy. His goal is to make his master happy; it is not service. Service is just the means, but the aim is to give happiness.

Where Self Ends, Service Begins

What is service? There is bathing, feeding, massaging the feet, etc. All these are physical. What is the intention behind offering service with the body, mind and wealth that is described in the scriptures? The aim is to give him pleasure. In other words, service is done for the Beloved's happiness. Say, your beloved does not want to eat right now, but you insist that he does. Or, he is thirsty and wants to drink water, and you feel it is the appropriate time for milk. Such actions are not service. Service is performed with his happiness in mind.

Suppose his foot hurts and you feel, 'How can I give up my service of massaging his feet? No one can take away my right to serve, so I will do it, no matter what.' No. This will not do. Service means to give him happiness. You may not have the capability to understand what will give him pleasure. This is a very subtle thing, which you will not be able to understand at this stage. The biggest difficulty is to know what will give your master pleasure at a particular time. This is possible only for someone who knows his inner thoughts and feelings. Therefore, no one can do actual service.

सेवाधर्म: परमगहनो योगिनामप्यगम्य:।

(Bhartrihari, *Nitishatakam* 10.47.60)

It is said that even the greatest yogis find it difficult to comprehend the principles of service. When you become Saints, you will be able to perform service properly, because you will have all the appropriate powers. At present, we do not know the desires of God or Guru at any given moment. Let us say that our Guru wants us to leave his presence to be in solitude, but we persist in sitting there. Due to hesitation, he does not say anything, but he is not happy. Without knowing the inner thoughts and feelings of the master, what can a soul do? For them, the Saints give this advice: 'Just follow the instructions of your master, but the condition is that you should do it joyfully, accepting it as your good fortune.'

Suppose the Guru asks you to stay out of the *satsanga* hall for three days because of your transgressions. You were not doing your *rupadhyana* and not following the rules of *sadhana*, for which you had left home to practise here. You were breaking the vow of silence by talking privately and in this way cheating your Guru and God. 'But so many others were talking too. Why was I singled out for punishment?' The moment you start thinking like this, you violate your vow of discipleship and suffer a downfall.

You should be overwhelmed at being singled out because it means that the Guru has a special eye on you and a special kinship with you, which he does not have with others. He has selected you to be punished, considering the others ineligible for his personal attention. You should therefore carry out his instructions joyfully. This is the definition of service, and it applies to any instruction.

Exalted Service

Disciple of Lord Buddha

A disciple of Lord Buddha went to him and said, 'I would like to disseminate your message; propagate your instructions all over the world.' Lord Buddha replied, 'Son, this is a fine idea, but do you know the nature of worldly people? They will abuse and insult you on hearing your instructions. Then what will you do?' 'Master, I will be thankful that they did not beat me. What harm comes out of mere words? I will reflect on these teachings of Yours.' 'And what if someone does beat you or physically assaults you?' 'I will be grateful that I did not get killed. I received ten to twenty blows to my body and felt pain, but what harm is there in that? I will get better in two to four days. Many people would take ten days or more to recover.' 'And what if a partially insane person does kill you?' 'Then I will think that this body has died infinite times serving a spouse, parents and children. Now, just this once, it has come to an end in the service of my Guru. What greater fortune can there be than this?'

One must leave the body anyway. When the greatest of sages and yogis must die, who are we to think that our bodies will live forever? This body is destined to turn into dust or be burnt, so if it perishes once in the service of the Guru, what greater fortune could there be? This is the first time in infinite lifetimes that the body has been used properly. Prior to this, the body was destroyed for this wretched world.

If you were to take account of how much time your mind, body and wealth have been devoted to your spiritual goals, what would you find? And how much time in your life has this body been used properly in the service of Guru and God? How much time have you spent thinking about them?

What percentage of your income acquired throughout your life has been given in charity for a divine cause? If you think honestly about it, you will see that it is only a minuscule percentage. Is this its proper use? Everything was being frittered away uselessly. And if your mind, body and wealth go to the wrong place, it is followed by punishment. 'He is considered a thief and will be punished in the not-too-distant future.' 'Did you give one-tenth of your earnings to charity?' 'No, I did not.' 'What have you thought about it?'

'Look at my earnings! How can I possibly give to charity?' 'Will you not leave this body?' 'Yes, I know that.' 'And you know that an account will be made of your actions?' 'Yes, I know that too.' 'And according to spiritual law, if you have not done what you should have, you will be punished.' 'I will see what happens.' That is the final argument. When will you see? It's not as if you know the time of your death. Your warrant could be issued at any moment. That time is not far off.

Actual service is a very exalted state in which there is no need for any instructions. In this state, you know the mind of your master; you know his desire at every moment and promptly execute it for his happiness. This is not within the capability of an ordinary soul.

Living by the Master's Will

Service for ordinary souls has therefore been described as 'Obedience to Instructions'. We should act according to our capabilities. When we surrender ourselves according to our capabilities, we please God and Guru. Even though it is not true service, they appreciate the fact that a soul is doing all it can in its power to surrender itself. No teacher expects a first-grade student to give answers like a student pursuing a master's degree. A student in the first grade is expected to know his multiplication tables from one to ten, and if someone has memorised it up to twelve, he is considered an intelligent boy for doing so. The teacher is happy and praises him for he has gone beyond course expectations. Now if another student says, 'But why are you commending him for that? I can do far more.' But he is being appreciated according to his level.

To keep our desires in line with our Guru is therefore difficult. If we are not able to please him, then the very least we can do is avoid giving him any displeasure. This is an ordinary concept that everyone can understand. If we cannot make him happy, then at least make sure that we do not make him unhappy with our behaviour. Otherwise, what is the sense of life if, having received a human body, it is not used for the ultimate goal? This mind, intellect and wealth are to be condemned if they are not put to their proper use, because they are causing harm by being misused. If something is not used properly, it is bound to be misused. This is the law of nature. Similarly, if your mind is not absorbed in Guru and God, it will run to the world. This is unavoidable. Everything keeps changing constantly, and the world is constantly changing too. It is temporary and destructible.

Understanding True Selflessness

Our goal, therefore, is to serve God without any trace of desire for our own happiness. There is a subtle point that should be carefully noted here. Some people innocently think that to end all desires means to no longer desire to see God, hear His words, smell His fragrance or experience His touch, because to desire the objects of the senses from God for one's own pleasure is wrong. To desire only God as the object of all the senses is compulsory. However, it should not be for your own happiness, but for His alone. These desires should increase every moment. 'When will I see Him?' This restlessness, this yearning, should constantly increase and never decrease. If it is not His desire to come today, tomorrow or within a year or in this lifetime, then there should be no objection on your part. Your love should not diminish and there should be no complaints from your side.

You must be ready to sacrifice yourself on this unfavourable behaviour. 'He is always with me, and He notes every tear I shed. But look at His naughtiness in not coming before me. Nevertheless, I will not lessen my love; rather, it will continue to grow steadily, whether He comes or not.' If it gives Him happiness not to come today, but tomorrow, then that is all right. There should just be an increase in the yearning from our side. In the world, this is totally opposite. If you are expecting some of your loved ones to visit and they arrive late, you can get upset and even develop feelings of hostility towards them. So be careful and avoid developing this kind of attitude in the spiritual field.

We must keep our desires connected to Him. If they come to an end, then what is left? If this was the goal, then all souls are Saints and selfless devotees. Where is the love? 'I do not shed tears for Shri Krishna, do *kirtan* or do *rupadhyana*.' 'Why?' 'If I meditate on Him, He will meditate on me and if I shed tears for Him, He will shed tears for me. I do not want Him to do this, so I will not love Him.' If an innocent person starts thinking like this, then all atheists are Saints of the highest order because they never take His name and so He never has to take theirs. Just as they are indifferent to Him, He is indifferent to them. No. You must increase your love.

You must yearn for Him like a lustful man yearns for the association of a woman, as a greedy man longs for money. Love is something that is ever-increasing and will continue to grow even after the attainment of God. This is not something you have to reduce, but it should not be for your happiness, just His. This subtle point needs to be noted.

12

My Beloved

GOD HAS INFINITE POWERS.

परास्य शक्तिर्विविधैव श्रूयते स्वाभाविकी ज्ञानबलक्रिया च।

(*Shvetashvatara Upanishad* 6.8)

The *Vedas* state that Shri Krishna has infinite powers; out of these powers, the foremost is His *para shakti*. Many synonyms are used for *para shakti* in the scriptures, including the *Vedas*. Somewhere, it is called *chit shakti*. The *Gita* calls it *atma-maya*. The *Bhagavatam* calls it *yogamaya*.

सम्भवाम्यात्ममायया (*Gita* 4.6)
योगमायामुपाश्रित: (*Bhagavatam* 10.29.1)

This is not *maya*. That is separate from *maya*. There are two types of *maya*. One is His personal power. You must have heard that God performs all His actions through *yogamaya*. This *yogamaya* or *atma-maya* or *chit shakti* or *para shakti*, is His personal power. The other is His external power, *maya*.

अजोऽपि सन्नव्ययात्मा भूतानामीश्वरोऽपि सन्।
प्रकृतिं स्वामधिष्ठाय सम्भवाम्यात्ममायया॥ (*Gita* 4.6)

Yogamaya is not the inert *maya* that holds sway over us in the material world. That *maya* is under *yogamaya* and cannot exist before it. Just as the sun is the cause of both light and darkness — but darkness cannot exist before light — similarly, God has two powers — *yogamaya* and *maya*. *Maya* cannot exist before *yogamaya*. This *maya* stays far away. This *para shakti* is the foremost of all powers of God.

The Glory of God's Powers

Para shakti has many effects, but mainly we can say there are two: (1) *svarupa parinama* and (2) *viruddha parinama*.

In *svarupa parinama*, the effect has all the qualities of the cause. When, for example, milk turns into yoghurt, it is a variation, a change from the original. Bacteria enters the milk and turns it into yoghurt. Milk does not remain milk anymore. Similarly, when the world emerges from God, this is an opposing effect because it is the work of *maya* and *maya* is an opposing power which has all the opposite qualities of God. The effect of *maya* is the opposing effect of God. But God remains as He is, in His own personality.

Therefore, there are two types of effects. One in which all the qualities are retained that are in God — just as His own abode, Goloka, is divine and non-different from Him. The earth, water, fire, air and ether there are all divine and of His nature. But in our world, all these things are material or *mayic*. Thus, from one God, two effects emanate: (1) the divine realm, Goloka, which is an effect having His own nature, *svarupa parinama*; and (2) the material (*mayic*) world, which is an opposing effect, *viruddha parinama*.

Nevertheless, Shri Krishna Himself remains unchanged. When milk becomes yoghurt, it is transformed and loses its identity, but this is not the case with Shri Krishna. These are (*vibhavas*) the effects of *para shakti*.

Along with this, *para shakti* has (*prabhavas*) three kinds of influences – *jnana*, *bala*, *kriya*. *Jnana* is knowledge, *bala* refers to desire and *kriya* refers to action. There are three recipients of their influence: (1) God, (2) the individual soul and (3) *maya*.

In God, knowledge is complete, and desire and action are found in an unlimited amount. In the individual soul, these three are seen in an infinitesimally small quantity; the soul has limited knowledge, limited desires and limited actions. And everything is the reverse in *maya;* there is nescience, no desire and it is inert.

There are (*anubhavas*) effects of those qualities, too. *Para shakti* has three *anubhavas* – *sat*, *chit* and *ananda*. Brahm is described as *sacchidananda (sat-chit-ananda)*.

The effect of *sat* is *sandhini shakti*, the effect of *chit* is *samvita shakti* and the effect of *ananda* is *hladini shakti*. These three also have the same qualities. I am not going to take you into too much depth. I will instead summarise everything in nine sentences. Be attentive!

1. From the *sandhini* part of Shri Krishna's *chit shakti*, the effects produced are His names, forms, pastimes or *lila*, qualities, abodes, etc.

2. From the *samvita* part of His *chit shakti*, one gets the experience of His opulence, *aishvarya*, His sweetness, *madhurya*, and His beauty, *saundarya*.

3. From the *hladini anubhava* of His *chit shakti*, the bliss of divine love, *premananda*, is obtained.

These were all the effects of Shri Krishna's personal power, His *chit shakti*. Now let us see the *jiva shakti* of which the soul is a part.

1. From the *sandhini shakti anubhava* of the *jiva shakti*, the soul acquires its eternal conscious existence, its name and its form as the effects.

2. From the *samvita anubhava* of the *jiva shakti*, the soul can acquire knowledge of Brahm, *brahmjnana*.

3. From the *anubhava* of the *hladini* part of the *jiva*, the soul attains liberation, *moksha* or the bliss of Brahm, *brahmananda*.

Now we move on to *maya*.

1. The third *shakti* is *maya*. From the *sandhini anubhava* of *maya*, the senses, mind, intellect and the name of the body are produced as effects.

2. From the *samvita anubhava* of *maya*, anxiety, grief, tension and various other afflictions arise as effects.

3. From the *hladini anubhava* of *maya shakti*, the pleasure of worldly relationships — spouse, parents, children, worldly objects — and the pleasure of the celestial abodes are experienced.

There are nine points in total, but only the first three are relevant to you.

1. From the *sandhini* part of Shri Krishna's *chit shakti*, His names, forms, qualities, pastimes and abodes are manifested.

2. From the *samvita shakti*, His opulence, His sweetness and His beauty are manifested.

3. From His *hladini shakti*, the bliss of divine love is manifested.

These three should be your only concern.

All these powers are the personal and confidential powers of Shri Krishna. Always remember and realise that these divine powers of your Beloved Shri Krishna are fully present in His holy names, divine qualities, enchanting forms, transcendental pastimes and eternal abodes. Therefore, focus your mind on these divine aspects and perform *rupadhyana* (meditative visualisation of His form) while engaging in *sankirtana* (devotional chanting). By doing so, you will find that your mind becomes attached very quickly.

Total Surrender in Love

Always remember that you must love Shri Krishna unselfishly and you must challenge Him. What is the challenge?

आश्लिष्य वा पादरतां पिनष्ट मामदर्शनान्मर्महतां करोतु वा।
यथा तथा वा विदधातु लम्पटो मत्प्राणनाथस्तु स एव नापर:॥

(Shikshashtaka)

O Shri Krishna! Whether You embrace me lovingly and
display Your affection as per the natural way of love, or
whether You act indifferently as though You have never seen
me before or whether You behead me with Your divine disc,
I give You complete freedom to do whatever, whenever,
wherever, and as much as it pleases You.

This is not said in anger, but in submission with love. 'Do whatever makes You happy. Your contrary behaviour will not reduce or finish my love for You. I am ready to sacrifice everything on every action of Yours, even if it is contrary in nature.' If you always and at all times adhere to this and make it firm in your mind, then your love will keep increasing with every passing moment and you will never face any danger. Danger arises when you have desires such as 'things should happen this way' or 'why is He not doing this'. The moment you apply your impure material intellect, everything is ruined.

You must make His desire your desire. He is all-knowing and all-powerful. He will give you the most appropriate instructions at the appropriate time. You just have to carry it out joyfully. And you should not ask Him for anything, because you do not have the intelligence to know what to ask from Him. Look at Hiranyakashipu. He used his intellect to ask for the boon not to be killed during the day or night, not inside or outside the house and not by any man or beast, and so on. But despite his long list of conditions, he was killed anyway. Your intellect has no access to the divine realm; you just have to surrender it.

In this way, you have found out from the Rasika Saints that God alone is yours. You must love Him following the conditions that have been explained to you, so that you do not fall into any danger before reaching the intended goal. Your love should keep on increasing until your mind is completely pure. If your mental attachment increases, your mind, which is the receptacle to receive divine love, will very quickly become ready. Once the receptacle is ready, you will receive divine love from the Guru, and thus attain the treasure you have been seeking.

प्राणधन जीवन कुंज बिहारी।
तुम तो रहे सनातन हमरे, हौं हूँ रही तिहारी।
उर लगाय भुज भरि हरि चाहे, पुरवहु आस हमारी।

चाहे मोहिँ तड़पाउ मोरि मुख, पग ठुकराव मुरारी।

जेहि विधि पिवु सुख पाउ करिय सोइ, मो कहँ सोइ सुख भारी।

यह 'कृपालु' है रीति प्रीति की, निज सुख चह व्यापारी॥

(*Prema Rasa Madira*, 'Siddhanta Madhuri' 3.64)

A *gopi* manifesting her selfless love for Shri Krishna says: 'O Krishna! You are the wealth of my life. You have eternally been mine and I am eternally Yours. Whether You fulfil my desire by taking me in Your arms and embracing me closely, or turn away from me, feigning indifference, thus tormenting me, or whether You kick me away as though renouncing me, Your pleasure and Your desire will always be mine too.'

Shri Kripalu Ji Maharaj reasserts, 'This is in fact the proper way to love. Love which seeks one's own happiness is mere business.'

Notes

1. THE TRUE RELATION

1. A month-long spiritual retreat that is held every year in Kripalu Dham Mangarh, the birthplace of Jagadguruttam Shri Kripalu Ji Maharaj.

2. THE MIND AND THE INTELLECT

1. Samkhya, one of the six classical schools of Indian philosophy, was founded by Sage Kapila and is known for its dualistic and rational approach to metaphysics.
2. The mind is focused on God and no longer desires any contact with the material world.

3. THE SPIRITUAL HURDLES

1. At a devotional retreat.
2. All objects associated with God, like His ornaments, weapons, etc., are divine personalities.

4. THE PATH OF SURRENDER

1. The world population in 1981.
2. Lord Shiva's weapon of final annihilation.

5. THE NATURE OF LOVE

1. An offence against God and the Saints; ill feeling or any negative attitude towards their names, forms, attributes, pastimes and abodes which nullifies the effects of devotional practice.
2. An anthology of classical poetry on devotion written by

Jagadguruttam Shri Kripalu, comprising 1,008 devotional songs. Visit www.jkpliterature.org.in for details.

3. The manifestation of Shri Krishna's highest form of divine love — bliss in the form of an amorous dance with Shri Radha and the *gopis*. Also called *maharaas*.

6. He Alone Is Mine

1. Bharata says this when he comes to Chitrakoot to persuade Rama to return to Ayodhya and take back the throne.
2. In 1981, during devotional retreats, there was the strict rule of observing the vow of silence and just uttering the names of God.
3. In the year 1981.

7. The Lover

1. Advocates of wilful restraint of the mind.
2. In 1981, during a devotional retreat.
3. Shri Maharaj Ji's speech in Sadhana Bhawan, 1981.

9. Desires and Love

1. The philosophy of God, the soul, and the world from A to Z, written by Jagadguruttam Shri Kripalu.
2. King Chitraketu, ruler of the Vidyadharas, had many wives but no children. Deeply distressed, he prayed for a son. Sage Angira visited him and blessed one of his queens to bear a son. The other queens, jealous and heartbroken, eventually poisoned the child, who died young. Chitraketu's joy turned to unbearable grief. (This story is cited to caution others not to be swayed by temporary pleasures at the cost of eternal spiritual progress.)

About Jagadguru Shri Kripalu Ji Maharaj

Shri Kripalu Ji Maharaj (5 October 1922–15 November 2013),
the fifth original Jagadguru in the history of the world.

JAGADGURU SHRI KRIPALU JI Maharaj was the only Saint of this age to be honoured with the title of Jagadguru, the highest authority among all Hindu Vedic Saints and scholars. This title is given only to that Saint who brings about a spiritual revolution in the world through his divine teachings. Jagadguru Shri Kripalu Ji Maharaj was the supreme exponent of Sanatan Dharm, the eternal Vedic religion, and his reconciliation of all the philosophies and faiths is unparalleled. Universally renowned as 'Bhaktiyoga-rasavatara', he was the pre-eminent Rasika Saint of this age, being the ultimate connoisseur of the nectar of divine love and ever absorbed in the blissful pastimes of Shri Radha–Krishna.

He appeared in 1922 on the auspicious night of Sharat Purnima, born into a highly respected Brahmin family in the remote village of Mangarh, in the district of Pratapgarh in Uttar Pradesh. He completed his early education in Mangarh and Kunda. Later, he studied Sanskrit grammar, literature and ayurveda at Indore, Chitrakoot and Varanasi.

At the tender age of sixteen, he retreated into the dense forests near the Sharbhang Ashram in Chitrakoot, and then into the forests near Vanshivat, Vrindavan. During that period, he was deeply engrossed in the divine love of Shri Radha–Krishna. Whoever saw him in that state of trance was astonished and felt that he was the very embodiment of love and bliss. Nobody at that time could have known that he had an unfathomable and immeasurably vast ocean of spiritual wisdom hidden within him. For the benefit of the people, he gradually started to conceal and control those ecstatic states in order to propagate the *bhakti* of Shri Krishna. Along with his inspiring messages of divine love, he started to reveal his divine wisdom and knowledge of the scriptures.

In 1955, Shri Maharaj Ji organised the first of two huge conferences in Chitrakoot, which was attended by all the Jagadgurus and other eminent scholars from Kashi (considered the seat of spiritual wisdom in India) and various other centres within India. The second conference took place in 1956, within the city of Kanpur. The most learned scholars of Kashi attending the conference were amazed to see such a young man possessing such scriptural omniscience. The most eminent and universally recognised scholar present, the chief secretary of the Kashi Vidvat Parishat (a body of 500 topmost scholars), Acharya Shri Raj Narayan Shatshastri, a leading luminary in the field of scriptural debate and a foremost philosopher of India, made a public proclamation after listening to Shri Maharaj Ji's discourse on 19 October 1956, a part of which is quoted below:

You are extremely fortunate to have in your midst a Saint who can present this level of divine knowledge. Kashi is the centre of spiritual learning for the entire world. We, the residents of Kashi, are seated here. Hearing Shri Kripalu Ji's divine utterances yesterday, we were all compelled to accept humble submission before him...

Kashi Vidvat Parishat invited Shri Maharaj Ji to address them in Kashi, which he did the following year.

The extraordinary discourses delivered by Shri Maharaj Ji in classical Sanskrit to the scholars of Kashi Vidvat Parishat, combined with his 'out of this world' personality, soaked in the bliss of divine love, left the learned gathering completely spellbound. They unanimously admitted that he was not only a great scholar of the *Vedas* and all other scriptures, but also an embodiment of divine love. They unanimously honoured him with several titles, including Jagadguru, declaring him to be Jagadguruttam, the supreme amongst all Jagadgurus.

This historic event took place on 14 January 1957, when Shri Maharaj Ji was just thirty-four years of age. Prior to him, only four Saints have been honoured with the title of Jagadguru: Adi Jagadguru Shri Shankaracharya, Jagadguru Shri Ramanujacharya, Jagadguru Shri Nimbarkacharya and Jagadguru Shri Madhvacharya.

For over fifty years, Shri Maharaj Ji delivered hundreds of enlightening discourses, effortlessly and eloquently reciting Sanskrit verses from the *Vedas, Puranas, Upanishads, Gita* and other scriptures, leaving both scholars and laypersons speechless. He revealed thousands of *bhajans* and *kirtanas* that evoke extremely devotional sentiments within the heart, while his literary works explain the philosophy of the *Vedas* and Vedic scriptures in a very simple, practical and logical manner. He personally trained preachers who travel the world spreading the most authentic divine wisdom contained in our scriptures. Together with his televised discourses, his teachings have now spread across the globe.

The spiritual work undertaken by Shri Maharaj Ji is certainly his greatest contribution to society. However, recognising the need to take care of the physical body, Shri Maharaj Ji inspired people to engage in humanitarian activities as well. Thus, the international, non-profit, charitable, educational and spiritual organisation, Jagadguru Kripalu Parishat, was established in 2002. Charitable institutions that serve the poor and needy in the areas of health and education are fully operational in some of India's most underdeveloped areas. Centres for devotional practice are scattered throughout India and abroad, providing venues for people to practise the principles of *bhaktiyoga* in their daily life.

Making no distinction between caste, creed, colour, race or religion, and with his infinite love and compassion, Shri Maharaj Ji gathered all into the purity of his divine embrace. His divine effulgence shone through all he said, all he did and all he was. Every seeker was amazed to see how approachable he was and enjoyed the special privilege of receiving attention from him. In so doing, he made everyone feel that they belonged to him. It is very easy to become a recipient, because there was no giver like Shri Maharaj Ji. True to his moniker, Kripalu, he was the very ocean of grace.

In this age, where people are judged by material success, the human soul yearning for peace and fulfilment finds soothing solace in Shri Maharaj Ji's unique philosophy. His teachings shatter all doubts of spiritual confusion with great ease and effectively reveal a clear and practical path leading to God.